Critical Challenges in English
for Secondary Students (Revised Edition)

A collection of 21 critical thinking lessons addressing a range of literary genres

Editors

Samantha Butler

Holly Husarski Mair

Shirleen Sayers

Nancy Shea

Authors

Samantha Butler

Muriel Densford

Suzanne Duke

David Ellison

Holly Husarski Mair

Larry Killick

Shani Laver

Gale Parchoma

Phylis Schwartz

Natasha Schroeter

Nancy Shea

Series Editors

Roland Case

LeRoi Daniels

The Critical
Thinking Consortium

Critical Challenges
ACROSS THE CURRICULUM

Series published by

The Critical Thinking Consortium
University of British Columbia
Education Building
6365 Biological Sciences Road
Vancouver, BC Canada V6T 1Z4
Fax: 604.822.6603
Tel: 604.822.9297
E-mail: tc2@interchange.ubc.ca
www.tc2.ca

Series distributed by

Pacific Educational Press
Faculty of Education
University of British Columbia
Vancouver, BC V6T 1Z4
Tel: 604.822.5385
Fax: 604.822.6603
www.pep.educ.ubc.ca

McGraw-Hill Ryerson, School Division
300 Water Street
Whitby, ON L1N 9B6
Tel: 905.430.5247
Fax: 905.430.5023
www.mcgrawhill.ca

Cover Design: Antonia Banyard

Interior Design: M. Kathie Wraight, Field Programs, Simon Fraser University

Production: M. Kathie Wraight, Field Programs, Simon Fraser University

Cover Photograph: Statue of Euripedes, Vatican Museum, Rome

The Critical Thinking Consortium is especially grateful to the **Vancouver Foundation** for its financial support of this resource and many of the other volumes in this series.

First edition, 1998

Second edition, 2007

Library and Archives Canada Cataloguing in Publication

Critical challenges in English for secondary students : a collection of 21 critical thinking lessons addressing a range of literary genres / authors, Samantha Butler ... [et al.] ; editors, Samantha Butler ... [et al.]. -- Rev. ed.

(Critical challenges across the curriculum series, ISSN 1205-9730)
ISBN 978-0-86491-257-2

1. English language--Study and teaching (Secondary) 2. Language arts (Secondary) I. Butler, Samantha, 1968- II. Critical Thinking Consortium. III. Series.

LB1631.C74 2007   428.0071'2   C2007-905225-8

Introduction

Critical Challenges

Table of Contents

Critical Challenges Across the Curriculum is an ongoing series of teacher resources focussed on infusing critical thinking into every school subject and at all levels. Two features distinguish this series from many other publications on critical thinking—our *curriculum embedded* approach and our emphasis on *teaching the intellectual tools*.

Our approach is to embed critical thinking by presenting focussed questions or tasks that invite critical student reflection about the content of the curriculum. We do not support the view of critical thinking as a set of generic skills or processes that can be developed independent of content and context. Nor do we believe that critical thinking can adequately be addressed as an add-on to the curriculum. Rather, if it is to take a central place in the classroom, critical thinking must be seen as a way of teaching the content of the curriculum. Teachers can help students understand the subject matter, as opposed to merely recall it, by providing continuing opportunities for thoughtful analysis of issues or problems that are central to the subject matter.

The second distinguishing feature of this series is our emphasis on systematically teaching the intellectual tools for critical thinking. Much of the frustration teachers experience when attempting to engage students in thinking critically stems from students' lack of the required concepts, attitudes, knowledge, criteria or strategies—in short, they lack the tools needed to do a competent job. It is often assumed that the mere provision of invitations to think will improve students' reflective competence. We believe that constructing a thoughtful response is like building a house in that it is impossible to do a competent job in either case unless one has the necessary tools. For this reason, each critical thinking challenge in the series includes a list of the tools needed to respond competently and, more importantly, activities suggesting how these tools may be taught.

We hope that teachers will find these resources of use in increasing and improving the teaching of critical thinking in their subject areas.

Roland Case & LeRoi Daniels

Series Editors

Most of the critical challenges in this collection were developed and piloted by secondary school teachers of the Okanagan Similkameen School District, British Columbia, between October 1996 and June 1997. An updating of the format and expansion of the assessment features of the original publication was undertaken by Shirleen Sayers in the summer and fall of 2004. In addition to the authors of the critical challenges, we would like to thank the following educators for their help in this project:

Darlene Abbie	Okanagan Similkameen School District
Lindsay Abbie	Okanagan Similkameen School District
Phyllis Schwartz	Vancouver School District

Special thanks goes to Superintendent Brian Fox for his initiative to bring the TC^2 critical thinking model to the Okanagan Similkameen School District for the district's leadership and financial support of this project. Our thanks to Catherine Edwards for the thoughtful editing of the revised edition.

Acknowledgements

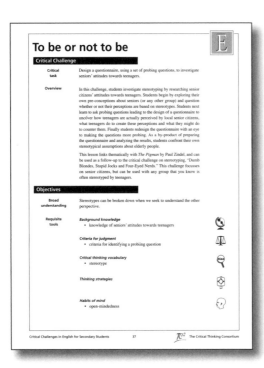

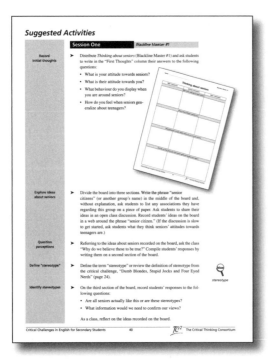

Each **critical challenge** opens with a **question** or **task** which is the focal activity upon which the lesson is based. An **overview** describes the topic and the main activities that students undertake.

Broad understanding is the intended curricular understanding that will emerge as students work through the challenge.

Requisite tools provides an inventory of specific intellectual resources that students need to competently address the critical challenge:

 Background knowledge — the information about the topic required for thoughtful reflection;

 Criteria for judgment — the considerations or grounds for deciding which of the alternatives is the most sensible or appropriate;

 Critical thinking vocabulary — the concepts and distinctions that help to think critically about the topic;

 Thinking strategies — procedures, organizers, models or algorithms that help in thinking through the challenge;

 Habits of mind — the values and attitudes of a careful and conscientious thinker that are especially relevant to the critical challenge.

The body of the lesson is found under **suggested activities** that indicate how the critical challenge may be introduced and how the requisite tools may be taught.

Where relevant, **sessions** indicate where each anticipated new lesson would begin and the blackline masters needed for that session.

Down the left-hand panel is a handy **summary of main tasks** or activities for each session.

Icons along the right-hand side point out where specific tools are addressed.

Also provided in **evaluation** are assessment criteria and procedures, and in **extension** are found suggestions for further exploration or broader application of key ideas.

References cited in the suggested activities or recommended for additional information are often listed.

Blackline masters *are found immediately after individual lessons or, in the case of a sequenced unit, at the back of the volume. These are the reproducible learning resources referred to in the suggested activities. They serve a wide range of purposes:*

- **assessment rubrics** *identify suggested criteria and standards for evaluating student work;*

- **briefing sheets** *provide background information for students;*

- **data charts** *contain various organizers for recording and analyzing information;*

- **documents** *refer to primary source material including paintings and other illustrations;*

- **student activities** *provide questions and tasks for students to complete;*

- **transparencies** *refer to material that can be converted to a transparency for use on an overhead projector.*

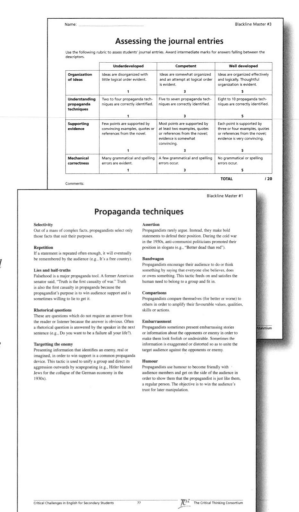

Electronic sourcebook *is a web-based supplement to our print publications. These materials include colour reproductions of pictures, primary documents, and updated links to other sites.*

- *If electronic resources had been developed at the time of publication, the available resources are referenced in the Suggested Activities.*

- *Periodically we update or supplement the print volumes with additional electronic information and resources.*

To locate referenced materials or to see whether new material has been developed, access our website and look for the title of this publication under the Electronic Sourcebook *heading* (*www.tc2.ca/pub/sourcebook*).

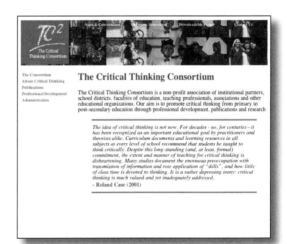

For more information about our model of critical thinking consult our website — www.tc2.ca.

Source materials appear in many of these lessons and may present a challenge to students. Below are four strategies to increase students' abilities and confidence in understanding difficult reading material.

Decoding foreign text

Encourage students to read documents as if they were written in a foreign language and need to be translated. This approach may be introduced in the following manner:

1. Write the following sentence on the board:

    Today's homework has been _____ due to an _____ on your teacher's part to _____ the assignment at home.

    Ask students to offer guesses as to what the full sentence might say.

2. Insert the following sets of words in the blank spaces.

    Today's homework has been *(1) cancelled (2) delayed (3) increased* due to an *(1) error (2) unwillingness (3) urge* on your teacher's part to *(1) verify (2) mark (3) burn* the assignment at home.

    Invite students to read out the first, second and third possibilities for this sentence.

3. Point out how the meaning changes dramatically depending on which words are inserted. The objective is to help students appreciate how badly they can be misled if they do not understand all the *key* terms in a passage.

4. Discuss strategies for helping students decode unknown words. A list could be posted in the classroom that includes the following:

    *   guess at its meaning and confirm that this interpretation makes sense in light of the rest of the sentence or passage;

    *   as a clue to its meaning, check whether the word resembles another word that is familiar (e.g., "benefactor" is similar to "benefit");

    *   look up the meaning in a dictionary or glossary;

    *   ask a fellow student or the teacher for help.

Team reading

Prepare students to work in teams to decode difficult passages by using a team reading activity:

1. Organize students into teams of two or three.

2. Assign students to read the document and ask team members the meanings of words that they do not understand; if no one on the team can explain the meaning of an unknown word, use a dictionary or ask the teacher for a definition.

3. After all team members have completed their reading, direct students to tell other team members what they think is the basic idea of the document. Once agreement has been reached, the team tells the teacher their agreed upon answer.

4. Ask students to look again at the document closely, perusing it for deeper meaning and identifying problematic areas; repeat the process of asking other team members or the teacher for clarification.

5. Finally, ask the team to prepare a précis that includes a two- or three-sentence summary of the essential meaning of the document, a theme statement and a conclusion.

SQ3R

The traditional SQ3R method (Survey, Question, Read, Recall, Review) provides a familiar procedure for some students. This method can be used in a team activity as outlined above or carried out as a class activity.

1. *Survey*: the teacher provides an overview of the topic addressed in the document.

2. *Question*: students pose questions that they have about the topic that may be addressed in the document before them.

3. *Read*: students read the document.

4. *Recall*: students share the main ideas of what they have just read.

5. *Review*: the teacher returns to the questions posed initially by students and discusses with the class any answers that may have been provided.

Graphic representation

Students often benefit from efforts to represent what they have learned by drawing key ideas. Presented below is a model for this approach.

1. Ask students to read the passage.

2. Invite students to sketch a picture of an image from the reading (or, in the case of longer passages, an assigned section) that they found particularly striking. Post their images in a collective grouping, providing students the opportunity to view the work of others.

3. Invite students to discuss in small groups what is contained in each picture and what it signifies.

Understanding critical thinking

Critical thinking involves thinking through problematic situations about what to believe or how to act where the thinker makes reasoned judgments that embody the qualities of a competent thinker.

A person is attempting to think critically when she thoughtfully seeks to assess what would be sensible or reasonable to believe or do in a given situation. The need to reach reasoned judgments may arise in countless kinds of problematic situations such as trying to understand a passage in a text, trying to improve an artistic performance, making effective use of a piece of equipment, or deciding how to act in a delicate social situation. What makes these situations problematic is that there is some doubt as to the most appropriate option.

Critical thinking is sometimes contrasted with problem solving, decision making, analysis and inquiry. We see these latter terms for rational deliberation as occasions for critical thinking. In all these situations, we need to think critically about the options. There is limited value in reaching solutions or making choices that are not sensible or reasonable. Thus, the term critical thinking draws attention to the quality of thinking required to competently pose and solve problems, reach sound decisions, analyze issues, plan and conduct thoughtful inquiries and so on. In other words, thinking critically is a way of carrying out these thinking tasks just as being careful is a way of walking down the stairs. Thus, thinking critically is not a unique *type* of thinking that is different from other types of thinking, rather it refers to the *quality* of thinking. The association of critical thinking with being negative or judgmental is misleading, since the reference to critical is to distinguish it from uncritical thinking—thinking that accepts conclusions at face value without any assessment of their merits or bases. It is more fruitful to interpret critical in the sense of critique—looking at the merits and shortcomings of alternatives in order to arrive at a reasoned judgment.

Our focus on the quality of thinking does not imply that students must arrive at a preconceived right answer, rather we look to see that their varied responses exhibit the qualities that characterize good thinking in a given situation. For example, it wouldn't matter whether students opposed or supported a position expressed in a newspaper or textbook. Regardless of their particular position, we would want students' critically thoughtful responses to exhibit sensitivity to any bias, consideration of alternative points of view, attention to the clarity of key concepts, and assessment of supporting evidence. We believe that emphasis on qualities that student responses should exhibit focuses teachers' attention on the crucial dimension in promoting and assessing students' competence in thinking critically. The challenge for teachers is to adopt practices that will effectively promote these qualities in their students.

Promoting critical thinking

To help students improve as critical thinkers, we propose a four-pronged approach:

- build a *community of thinkers* within the school and classroom;
- infuse opportunities for critical thinking—what we call *critical challenges*—throughout the curriculum;
- develop the *intellectual tools* that will enable students to become competent critical thinkers;
- on a continuing basis *assess students' competence* in using the intellectual tools to think through critical challenges.

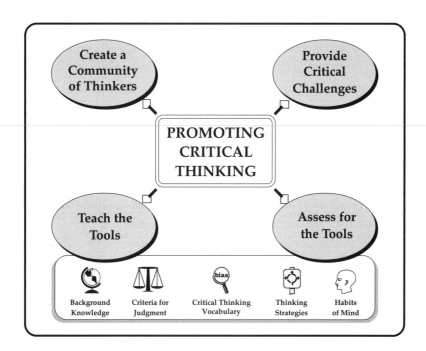

Building a community of thinkers

Developing supportive school and classroom communities where reflective inquiry is valued may be the most important factor in nurturing critical thinking. Many of the intellectual resources, or "tools" of critical thinking will not be mastered by students unless their use is reinforced on an ongoing basis. As well, the image of the thinker as a solitary figure is misleading. No one person can perfectly embody all the desired attributes—we must learn to rely on others to complement our own thoughts. There are many routines and norms that teachers can adopt to create a community of thinkers:

- Regularly pose questions and assignments requiring students to think through, and not merely recall, what is being learned.

- Creating ongoing opportunities to engage in critical and cooperative dialogue—confer, inquire, debate and critique—is key to creating a community of thinkers.

- Employ self- and peer-evaluation as ways of involving students in thinking critically about their own work.

- Model good critical thinking practices. Students are more likely to learn to act in desired ways if they see teachers making every effort to be open-minded, to seek clarification where needed, to avoid reaching conclusions based on inadequate evidence, and so on.

Infusing critical challenges throughout the curriculum

If students are to improve their ability to think critically, they must have numerous opportunities to engage and think through problematic situations—what we refer to as *critical challenges*.

- *Does the question or task require judgment?* A question or task is a critical challenge only if it invites students to assess the reasonableness of plausible options or alternative conclusions. In short, it must require more than retrieval of information, rote application of a strategy, uninformed guessing or mere assertion of a preference.

- *Will the challenge be meaningful to students?* Trivial, decontextualized mental exercises often alienate or bore students. It is important to frame challenges that are likely to engage students in tackling questions and tasks that they will find meaningful.

- *Does the challenge address key aspects of the subject matter?* Critical thinking should not be divorced from the rest of the curriculum. Students are more likely to learn the content of the curriculum if they are invited to think critically about issues embedded in the subject matter.
- *Do students have the tools or can they reasonably acquire the tools needed to competently address the challenge?* Students need support in acquiring the essential tools required to competently meet the critical challenge.

Developing intellectual tools for thinking critically

The key to helping students develop as critical thinkers is to nurture competent use of five types of tools of thinking. These categories of tools are *background knowledge*, *criteria for judgment*, *critical thinking vocabulary*, *thinking strategies* and *habits of mind*.

	Background Knowledge *—the information about a topic required for thoughtful reflection*	Students cannot think deeply about a topic if they know little about it. Two questions to ask in developing this tool: • What background information do students need for them to make a well-informed judgment on the matter before them? • How can students be assisted in acquiring this information in a meaningful matter?
	Criteria for Judgment *—the considerations or grounds for deciding which of the alternatives is the most sensible or appropriate*	Critical thinking is essentially a matter of judging which alternative is sensible or reasonable. Students need help in thinking carefully about the criteria to use when judging various alternatives. • Is my estimate *accurate*? • Is the interpretation *plausible?* • Is the conclusion *fair* to all? • Is my proposal *feasible*?
	Critical Thinking Vocabulary *—the range of concepts and distinctions that are helpful when thinking critically*	Students require the vocabulary or concepts that permit them to make important distinctions among the different issues and thinking tasks facing them. These include the following: • inference and direct observation; • generalization and over generalization; • premise and conclusion; • bias and point of view.
	Thinking Strategies *—the repertoire of heuristics, organizing devices, models and algorithms that may be useful when thinking through a critical thinking problem*	Although critical thinking is never simply a matter of following certain procedures or steps, numerous strategies are useful for guiding one's performance when thinking critically: • *Making decisions:* Are there models or procedures to guide students through the factors they should consider (e.g., a framework for issue analysis or problem solving)? • *Organizing information:* Would a graphic organizer (e.g., webbing diagrams, Venn diagrams, "pro and con" charts) be useful in representing what a student knows about the issue? • *Role taking:* Before deciding on an action that affects others, should students put themselves in the others' positions and imagine their feelings?
	Habits of Mind *—the values and attitudes of a careful and conscientious thinker*	Being able to apply criteria and use strategies is of little value unless students also have the habits of mind of a thoughtful person. These include: • *Open-minded:* Are students willing to consider evidence opposing their view and to revise their view should the evidence warrant it? • *Fair-minded:* Are students willing to give impartial consideration to alternative points of view and not simply impose their preference? • *Independent-minded:* Are students willing to stand up for their firmly held beliefs? • *Inquiring or "critical" attitude:* Are students inclined to question the clarity of and support for claims and to seek justified beliefs and values?

Assessing for the tools

Assessment is an important complement to the teaching of the tools of critical thinking. As suggested by the familiar adages "What is counted counts" and "Testing drives the curriculum," evaluation has important implications for what students consider important and ultimately what students learn. Evaluations that focus exclusively on recall of information or never consider habits of mind fail to assess, and possibly discourage, student growth in critical reflection.

A key challenge in assessing critical thinking is deciding what to look for in a student's answer. If there is no single correct response, we may well ask: "On what basis, then, can we reliably assess students?" In the case of critical thinking, we would want to see how well students exhibited the qualities of a competent thinker. Thus, the intellectual resources or tools for critical thinking become the criteria for assessing students' work. The following example suggests each of the five types of critical thinking tools and specific assessment criteria that might be considered when evaluating critical thinking in an argumentative essay and an artistic work.

Type of criteria for assessment	Evidence of critical thinking in a persuasive essay	Evidence of critical thinking in an artistic work
Background Knowledge *Has the student provided adequate and accurate information?*	• cited accurate information.	• revealed knowledge of the mechanics of the medium.
Criteria for Judgment *Has the student satisfied relevant criteria for judgment?*	• provided ample evidence; • arranged arguments in logical sequence.	• work was imaginative; • work was clear and forceful.
Critical Thinking Vocabulary *Has the student revealed understanding of important vocabulary?*	• correctly distinguished "arguments" from "counter arguments."	• represented "point of view."
Thinking Strategies *Has the student made effective use of appropriate thinking strategies?*	• used appropriate strategies for persuasive writing.	• employed suitable rehearsal/preparation strategies.
Habits of Mind *Has the student demonstrated the desired habits of mind?*	• demonstrated an openness to alternative perspectives; • refrained from forming firm opinions where the evidence was inconclusive.	• was open to constructive criticism; • demonstrated a commitment to high quality; • demonstrated a willingness to take risks with the medium.

One of the objectives in the study of literature is to develop students' ability to think critically—to forumulate their own thoughtful opinions rather than to naively accept the ideas of others' at face value. This means that they must acquire the "tools" to think and communicate competently and intelligently. This collection of 21 critical challenges introduces a range of the key tools that middle and secondary school students require for thinking about various literary genres. In many cases the lessons are self-contained and can be taught independently; others must be part of a larger unit of study about a play or novel.

Suggested grade levels

M = Middle School   **S = secondary school**   **M/S = both middle and secondary school**

Novels

 A **Death by association**

2 sessions

M

In this critical challenge, students determine who is most responsible for the death of Johnny Cade, a character from S.E. Hinton's novel *The Outsiders*. Johnny suffers many injustices, and due to a series of unfortunate incidents, he eventually dies. Students are shown how to diagram interdependent contributing factors to an event and then use this strategy to assist them in determining which three characters are most responsible for Johnny's death.

 B **Would the real Dallas please stand up?**

2 sessions

M

In this critical challenge, students look at Dallas, a character from S.E. Hinton's novel *The Ousiders*, and draw inferences from his words and actions to reveal his personal qualities. Another character, Johnny, describe Dallas as "gallant". Although Dallas is a juvenile delinquent, Johnny compares him to the confederate soldiers in the novel *Gone with the Wind*. Students define the word "gallant" and compile evidence from the novel to determine whether or not Dallas is gallant. Students defend their position in a three-paragraph paper.

C **Who should we believe?**

2 sessions

M

In this critical challenge, students investigate the points of view of two narrators in Paul Zindel's novel *The Pigman*, to determine which narrator, John or Lorraine, provides a more credible account of events. The novel alternates between the two narrators, and as the point of view shifts, the reader is left wondering which character is more credible. Students complete a chart to analyze incidents reported differently by the narrators, and identify criteria for establishing the credibility of an account. The challenge concludes with a U-shaped discussion where students defend their assessment of the more reliable narrator.

D **Dumb blondes, stupid jocks and four-eyed nerds**

4 sessions

M

In this critical challenge, students explore the concept of stereotyping and develop strategies to break down stereotypes. The challenge is based on the novel *The Pigman* by Paul Zindel which contains many examples of stereotyping. After reading the novel, students brainstorm and discuss several examples of stereotyping found in *The Pigman*. They then look for stereotyping in their everyday world and the media. Finally, students work together to offer ways to dissolve stereotypes.

E **To be or not to be**

4 sessions

M

In this critical challenge, students investigate stereotyping by researching senior citizens' attitudes towards teenagers (or some other group that is often stereotyped by teengers). Students begin by exploring their own pre-conceptions about seniors (or another group) and question whether or not their perceptions are based on stereotypes. Students next learn to ask probing questions leading to design of a questionnaire to uncover how teenagers are actually perceived by local senior citizens, what teenagers do to create these perceptions and what they might do to counter them. Finally students redesign the questionnaire with an eye to making the questions more probing. As a by-product of preparing the questionnaire and analyzing the results, students confront their own stereotypical assumptions about elderly people.

This lesson links thematically with *The Pigman* by Paul Zindel and can be used as a follow-up to the critical challenge on stereotyping, "Dumb Blondes, Stupid Jocks and Four-Eyed Nerds" (Critical Challenge D).

F	**Should it stay or go?** 2 sessions	**M/S**	Every teacher has been faced with the question: "Why are we studying this novel?" This challenge invites students to work through this question. *My Left Foot*, by Christy Brown, a novel suitable for senior high students, is used as an example, but this approach could be adapted to evaluate at any grade level. Students determine criteria for selecting curriculum resources and then test a novel against these criteria, defending their position in a formal letter to the provincial Ministry of Education.
G	**Like a rolling stone** 2 sessions	**S**	In this challenge, students must decide whether or not Jack, Ralph or Roger, characters in the novel *Lord of the Flies* by William Golding, deserve to be charged with a homicide offense. This novel offers a scathing look at human nature and society. In it, a physically unappealing character named Piggy is killed by a group of boys who have become uncivilized. Students review the legal definitions of the terms manslaughter, first degree murder and second degree murder, and collect evidence from the novel to determine whether Jack, Ralph or Roger should be charged with a homicide offense, and if so, which offense.
H	**Leader of the pack** 2 sessions	**S**	This is the first of two challenges that use William Golding's novel *Lord of the Flies* as a springboard from which to investigate leadership qualities. In this challenge, students explore the attributes of good leaders and assess whether two main characters in the novel, Ralph and Jack, possess these attributes. Students then judge which of these characters has the stronger leadership qualities.
I	**Who said words can't kill you?** 2 sessions	**S**	This is the second of two challenges about leadership based on William Golding's novel *Lord of the Flies*. In this challenge, students learn that the characters who possess the strongest leadership qualities do not necessarily become the most powerful leaders, and that this is also true in real life. Often leaders find ways to become powerful to make up for their leadership deficiencies. Students examine how power can be acquired by using propaganda techniques. They examine the behaviour of Ralph and Jack, the primary leaders in the novel, and study how they use propaganda techniques to enhance their natural leadership skills. Students conclude their analysis by selecting the more effective manipulator in the novel and writing a response journal entry explaining their choice.

Short Stories

J	**A question of pride?** 2 sessions	**M**	In this challenge, students explore the complex array of conflicting arguments that the protagonist Al Condraj must consider when making a moral decision in the short story *The Parsley Garden* by William Saroyan. The plot involves a young man from a low income, single parent family who steals a hammer. He feels ashamed and humiliated by his action and, after working off his debt, he is faced with the choice to continue working and swallow his pride, or to continue his meager way of living and keep his value system intact. Students make a judgment about Al's decision not to take a job. They then learn to make counter-arguments before they re-evaluate their initial assessment of Al's decision.
K	**Who done it?** 3 sessions	**M**	In this challenge, students examine the available evidence and decide whether Moose Maddon's death was accidental or murder. They then write an epilogue to *The Moose and the Sparrow*, a story by Hugh Garner, which expresses their opinion. In this story, Cecil is a slight young man who works at a logging camp during his summer breaks from university. Despite his pleasing personality and strong work ethic, Cecil is constantly tormented by Moose Maddon—a man who seems to be threatened by Cecil's intelligence. Moose has an unfortunate mishap and it is uncertain whether Moose's death was accidental or whether Cecil is responsible.

Daytime friends are night time lovers **M**

2 sessions

In this challenge, students examine the ambiguity created by Sinclair Ross in his short story, *The Painted Door*. This story concerns a couple who are facing marital difficulty. Ann, the wife, is attracted to her husband's friend, Steven. As the story progresses Sinclair Ross is deliberately ambiguous about Ann's fidelity. Students discuss what it means to be unfaithful and then examine Ann's fidelity or lack thereof. By doing this, students also learn more about counter-argument. In the culminating activity students write two diary entries from Ann's point of view: one which points to her infidelity and the other which points to her fidelity.

Poems

 Baseball is life . . . the rest is just details **M**

2 sessions

In this critical challenge, students explore the idea that a poem can serve as an extended metaphor. *The Base Stealer*, a poem by Robert Francis ostensibly describes a crucial type of play in baseball. It can also be read as a metaphor for many other things—life, decision-making and growing up. Students read the poem with the title removed, hypothesize what it is about, and them explore the effectiveness of the poem as an extended metaphor. They do this by looking for parallels between the poem and life, and by assessing the metaphor in light of agreed-upon criteria.

 Pushing the poetic envelope **M/S**

2 sessions

In this challenge, students explore concrete poetry—a form of poetry that arranges words to create a visual picture that enhances the poem's impact. Students consider a definition of poetry and the boundaries of poetic form, and learn how at times in the past, poetic form has been more rigidly defined. They explore how the visual arrangement of a poem can contribute to and enhance or even create its meaning. Ultimately, students author their own concrete poem.

Plays

 Back to the future **M/S**

2 sessions

In this two-part challenge, students evaluate the degree to which the themes explored in *A Midsummer Night's Dream* (or another Shakespearean play) are applicable to their own lives. Students begin by identifying the themes in a selected Shakespearean play and contemporary society. They create a collage to represent this relationship using newspapers and magazines. Finally they judge which of the themes found in the play is most relevant to modern society.

 Fate or free will? **M**

2 sessions

In this critical challenge, students assess the extent to which Romeo and Juliet are victims of fate rather than the authors of their own misfortune. Shakespeare's *Romeo and Juliet* is a romantic tragedy that focuses on the lives of two teenagers from feuding families who meet and fall in love. The long-standing feud between their families makes a relationship between these two lovers highly problematic, and a sequence of events unfolds in the play which leads to their tragic deaths. Students consider to what degree these events were caused by fate (circumstances beyond their control) or by free will (the result of their own decisions).

"Quote, unquote" **M/S**

2 sessions

In this two-part critical challenge, students select quotations to include an end-of-unit literature test that will ask them to identify the passage and analyze its significance. This challenge can be adapted for use at any grade level with any piece of literature. This particular lesson focuses on Shakespeare's *Macbeth*. Students explore the criteria for determining significant literary passages and then search an assigned part of the text looking for two quotations that satisfy these criteria. The class then judges the best among those quotes for inclusion in a culminating test for the unit.

R	**The nobler character: Laertes or Hamlet?** 2 sessions	**S**

In this challenge, students judge which of Laertes or Hamlet shows greater nobility of character. Shakespeare frequently employed characters to serve as foils in his plays. A foil is a character who, by contrast with the protagonist, underscores or enhances the distinctive characteristics of the protagonist. In *Hamlet*, Ophelia's brother Laertes is a foil for Hamlet. Students examine which Laertes circumstances are similar to those of Hamlet, and how the two characters react differently to similar circumstances. They consider the features of noble behaviour and then decide whether Hamlet or Laertes has a nobler character.

Essays

 Honesty: Is it the best policy?

2 sessions

S

In this challenge, students explore the act of cheating. Andrea Chisholm's essay "The 'High' of an Honest Win" examines the question of cheating, and more particularly, whether cheating is harmful to both the individual who cheats and the society to which he or she belongs. Students complete a pre-questionnaire about their attitudes towards cheating, and then investigate more deeply what it means to cheat. They read Chilsholm's essay, explore the reasons for and against cheating and write a brief essay on in response to Chilsholm's essay.

Songs

 Punctuating the lyrics

1 session

M/S

In this challenge, students consider how the Indigo Girls' song "Galileo," (or another appropriate song) written entirely in lower case letters without any punctuation, presents a unique punctuation task. The song is difficult to follow on paper, and is therefore an effective demonstration of the importance of punctuation. Students listen to the song to hear punctuation clues, add the punctuation marks they detect to the text of the song lyrics, and rewrite the lyrics with the punctuation added. They explain their choice of punctuation.

Fairy Tales

 On the other hand

2 sessions

M/S

In this two-part challenge, students shift the point of view of a fairy tale to that of a secondary character and rewrite the story from this perspective. They begin by hearing a revised version of a classic fairy tale – possibly *The Frog Prince Continued* (Jon Scieszka's rewrite of "The Frog Prince") or *The True Story of the Three Little Pigs! By A. Wolf* (Jon Scieszka's rewrite of "The Three Little Pigs"). After discussing the notion of point of view and the techniques writers use to alter point of view, students identify criteria for an effective "rewrite" of a fairy tale. They use these criteria to assess the effectiveness of the published revision before they rewrite a different fairy tale.

Death by association

Critical question

Which three characters are most responsible for Johnny's death?

Overview

In this critical challenge, students determine who is most responsible for the death of Johnny Cade, a character in S.E. Hinton's novel *The Outsiders*. Johnny suffers many injustices, and due to a series of unfortunate incidents, he eventually dies. Students are shown how to diagram interdependent contributing factors to an event and then use this strategy to assist them in determining which three characters are most responsible for Johnny's death.

Objectives

Broad understanding

Many events are caused by multiple, interdependent factors.

Requisite tools

Background knowledge
- familiarity with the novel *The Outsiders*

Criteria for judgment
- criteria for assigning responsibility (e.g., directly affected result, should have known better, acted freely, realistic to expect)

Critical thinking vocabulary

Thinking strategies
- diagram interdependent events

Habits of mind

Suggested Activities

Introduce hypothetical scenario

➤ To introduce the idea that events can be interdependent, begin with an example of a hypothetical but plausible local incident. The purpose of the exercise is to identify the groups/individuals who may have contributed directly and indirectly to this incident. The following scenario could be used as an example:

> A group of teens who like to skateboard have been kicked out of a store's parking lot because of an increase in litter and vandalism to the store in the form of a large, elaborate skateboard symbol spray-painted on the back of the building.

Identify direct contributing factors

➤ Using *Interdependent events* (Blackline Master #1) as an overhead, or as a sample for creating your own diagram, walk students through a few of the factors that contributed to the incident. Start with the Final Event (teens being kicked out of a parking lot) and identify the factors that contributed most directly to it. Once the obvious individuals and contributing events have been plotted on the diagram, trace the indirect contributing factors that influenced these direct direct factors.

interdependent events diagram

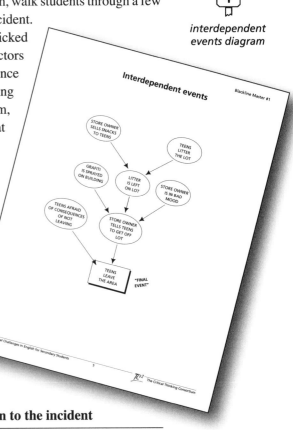

Identify indirect contributing factors

➤ Brainstorm suggestions for less obvious possibilities and record on a chart ways in which other individuals may have contributed to the turn of events. For the skateboard incident, the chart might look like the following:

Individuals involved	Contribution to the incident
parents	• did not provide supervision
	• did not establish guidelines for dealing with right and wrong actions
community	• did not provide a skateboard park
	• did not provide opportunities for constructive activities for teens
local merchants	• allowed the teens to use their lot
teens	• made lots of noise and acted irresponsibly

Work on diagrams in groups	➤ Divide students into small groups and ask each group tp prepare a final events diagram for the hypothetical incident by plotting how all individuals identified in the chart above and in the initial diagram may have contributed to the final event. Encourage students to add to the list of individuals and contributing factors as they complete their diagram. Ask each group to consider which individuals should be considered most responsible for the final event and why they think so.
Compile class diagram	➤ After each group has had an opportunity to develop their own diagram, create a collective interdependent events diagram. Invite each group to contribute some aspect to the diagram. Encourage students to see the interdependence of events and the multiple factors that contribute to any single incident. Close the activity by discussing with the class which individuals are most responsible for the final incident.

Session Two

<table>
<tr>
<td>Link to
The Outsiders</td>
<td>➤ Connect the idea of interdependent factors discussed in Session One to The Outsiders by asking students to list the names of all the characters in the novel who might have played a part in Johnny's death. Ask students to find quotations in the novel (noting page numbers) that provide evidence to support the hypothesis that this character was in some way responsible for Johnny's death.</td>
<td>
familiarity with the novel</td>
</tr>
<tr>
<td>Create an interdependent events diagram</td>
<td>➤ Ask students to diagram this information on an interdependent events diagram—as they did for the skateboard incident—to indicate how members of the community may have contributed to Johnny's death. Ask students to include quotes and page references on this diagram. Pairs of students should compare and discuss their diagrams and, where needed, refine and add to them.</td>
<td>
interdependent events diagram</td>
</tr>
<tr>
<td>Establish criteria</td>
<td>➤ Explore with the class the basis for deciding upon degrees of responsibility. Invite students to consider various factors including the following:

• Did the actions *directly affect the outcome*? (We are likely to diminish responsibility if there are many intervening events that need not have led to the eventual outcome.)

• Were the actions *deliberate and freely chosen*? (We often excuse those who had no choice in the matter—for example, actions done in self-defence.)

• Should the individual(s) *have known better*? (We are likely to hold a parent responsible for a young child that causes damage with a dangerous object because we think that parents, but not young children, should know better than to allow children to come in contact with dangerous objects.)</td>
<td>
criteria for assigning responsibility</td>
</tr>
<tr>
<td>Present the critical challenge</td>
<td>➤ Present the critical question:

Which three characters are most responsible for Johnny's death?</td>
<td></td>
</tr>
</table>

Explain the task

➤ Assign students a two-page essay in which they identify the three characters they hold to be most responsible for Johnny's death. Their view should be supported with detailed textual evidence selected using the previously-discussed criteria for assigning responsibility.

Evaluation
Blackline Masters #2-3

Assess the interdependent events diagram

➤ Assess the interdependent events diagram using the rubric *Assessing the diagram* (Blackline Master #2). According to the rubric, the assignment is worth 10 marks and is evaluated on the following criteria:

- identifies many of the actions that may plausibly be seen to contribute to Johnny's death;

- clearly represents the interdependence of contributing factors.

Assess the essay

➤ Assess the essays using the rubric *Assessing the position paper* (Blackline Master #3). According to the rubric, the assignment is worth 20 marks and is based on four criteria:

- clearly expresses the student's position on the responsible characters;

- identifies the criteria used as the basis for the conclusion;

- offers ample evidence in relation to each criterion to support the conclusion;

- is technically proficient with complete sentences, cohesive paragraphs and proper spelling and punctuation.

Extension

Apply to other selections

➤ Adapt this lesson to analyze the contributing cause of deaths in other works of literature such as *Romeo and Juliet, Macbeth* or *Julius Caesar*.

Diagram current events

➤ Invite students to use the interdependent events diagram to plot the factors that contribute to a topical event reported in the media.

Reference

Hinton, S.E. (1995). *The Outsiders*. New York: Puffin Books.

TC^2 The Critical Thinking Consortium

Interdependent events

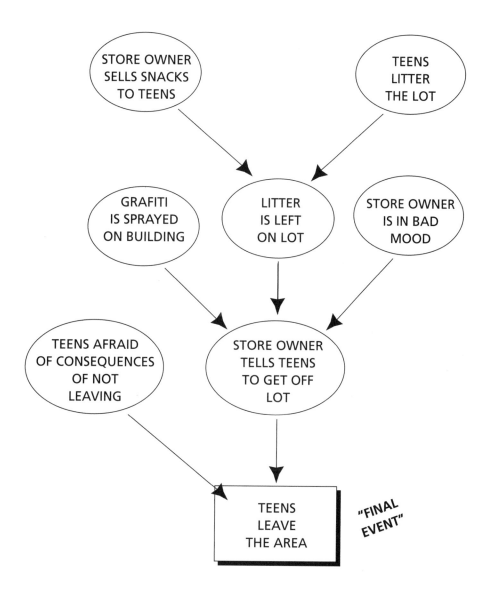

Assessing the diagram

Use the following rubric to assess students' identification of the interdependent actions associated with the final outcome. Award intermediate marks for answers falling between the descriptors.

	Underdeveloped	**Competent**	**Well developed**
Identifies plausible actions	Identifies very few plausible actions associated with the final outcome. 1	Identifies a number of plausible actions associated with the final outcome, but omits some important ones. 3	Identifies many plausible actions associated with the final outcome, including all of the most important contributing actions. 5
Represents causal inter-connections	Represents very few of the causal connections among the actions or misrepresent the relationships. 1	Represents a number of causal connections among the actions, but misrepresents some importants ones or misses the interdependent nature of some of the actions. 3	Represents many inter-dependent causal connections among the actions, including all of the most important connections. 5

Total   **/10**

Comments:

Assessing the paper

Use the following rubric to assess students' position papers. Award intermediate marks for answers falling between the descriptors.

	Underdeveloped	Competent	Well developed
Clearly states a position	No clear position is expressed on the question asked. **1**	Offers a position that only partly addresses the question asked. **3**	Very clearly and succinctly expresses a position that directly addresses the question asked. **5**
Identifies relevant criteria	Makes no obvious reference to the criteria used as the basis for reaching the conclusion. **1**	Identifies some criteria for reaching the conclusion, but key factors are ignored. **3**	Identifies all the key criteria used as the basis for reaching the conclusion. **5**
Offers ample evidence	Offers no relevant evidence from the text. **1**	Offers one piece of plausible evidence from the text for each criterion. **3**	Offers three or more very plausible pieces of evidence from the text for each criterion. **5**
Proficient at technical aspects	Writing may be ungrammatical, contain many spelling errors, and lack cohesive paragraphs and logical structure. **1**	Writing is generally technically correct with well structured paragraphs, but may contain minor grammatical or spelling errors. **3**	Writing is technically strong with correct grammar and accurate spelling, and cohesive, clear paragraphs. **5**

Total   /20

Comments:

Would the real Dallas please stand up?

Critical Challenge

Critical question

Is Dallas gallant?

Overview

In this critical challenge, students look at Dallas, a character from S.E. Hinton's novel *The Outsiders,* and draw inferences from his words and actions to reveal his personal qualities. Another character, Johnny, describes Dallas as "gallant." Although Dallas is a juvenile delinquent, Johnny compares him to the Confederate soldiers in the novel *Gone with the Wind*. Students define the word "gallant" and compile evidence from the novel to determine whether or not Dallas is gallant. Students defend their position in a three-paragraph paper.

Objectives

Broad understanding

Although gallantry is an old-fashioned concept not much considered today, it can still be found in modern behaviour—sometimes in unlikely circumstances.

Requisite tools

Background knowledge
- familiarity with the novel *The Outsiders*
- definition of gallantry

Criteria for judgment
- criteria for a plausible interpretation (e.g., plausible inferences, relevant evidence)

Critical thinking vocabulary
- inference

Thinking strategies
- data chart

Habits of mind

TC² The Critical Thinking Consortium

Suggested Activities

Use as culminating activity

➤ This lesson is designed as a culminating activity after students have finished reading S.E. Hinton's novel *The Outsiders*.

familiarity with the novel

Define "gallant"

➤ Ask students to define the word "gallant" and discuss the meaning as a class. You may wish to refer to the dictionary definition of gallant: nobility of spirit or action, courage; polite and attentive to women.

definition of gallant

List gallant people and actions

➤ Ask students to compile a list of people they consider to be gallant, using the primary definition of the word. At the junior high level, it may be easier to begin this list by naming gallant people from the school and community or from movies students have seen. Once this list is compiled, ask students to provide examples of gallant actions for each individual on the list.

Identify relevant information from novel

➤ Have students read the passage from *The Outsiders* (page 68), that describes Dallas as a gallant character. Ask students to describe Dallas' actions and Johnny and Ponyboy's interpretations of them. It might be helpful to diagram this information for the students as follows:

inference

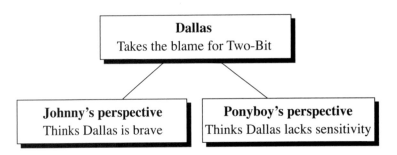

Dallas
Takes the blame for Two-Bit

Johnny's perspective
Thinks Dallas is brave

Ponyboy's perspective
Thinks Dallas lacks sensitivity

Session Two   *Blackline Master #1*

Define infer and inference

➤ Define and introduce the concept of inference. Ask students to consider possible inferences that could be drawn from Dallas' action, in addition to those of Johnny and Ponyboy. It might be helpful to offer examples to begin this activity:

- Dallas wants Two-Bit to like him.
- Dallas wants to be blamed for the vandalism.

Develop criteria for plausible inference

➤ Compile a class list of inferences and discuss which of these inferences are the most plausible in light of Dallas' other actions in the novel. Once class consensus is reached and students have a good grasp of the concept of a plausible inference, ask pairs of students to complete *Is Dallas gallant?* (Blackline Master #1).

data chart

Assess and revise inferences

➤ Once the blackline master is completed, ask students to discuss which inference(s) is (are) most consistent with the rest of the text and identify those inference(s) on Blackline Master #1 using a highlighter pen.

consistent or plausible interpretation

Pose the critical question

➤ When this task is completed, ask students to report their decisions in a class discussion and conclude by discussing Dallas' character traits with the class. After the discussion, pose the critical question:

Is Dallas gallant?

Ask students to write a three-paragraph position paper in which they define gallantry and argue whether or not Dallas is gallant, using evidence from the class discussion and the novel. Encourage students to connect their evidence to the identified criteria for gallantry.

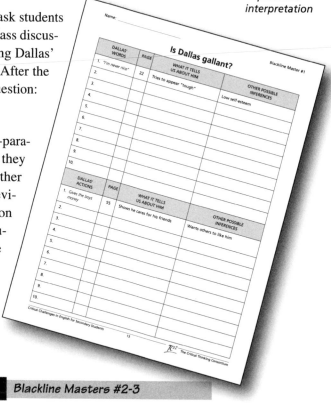

Evaluation
Blackline Masters #2-3

Assess the data chart

➤ Assess the data chart using the rubric *Assessing the inferences* (Blackline Master #2. According to the rubric, the assignment is worth 15 marks and is evaluated on the following criteria:

- identifies relevant references in the text to Dallas' actions and statements;
- offers interesting alternative inferences for each reference.

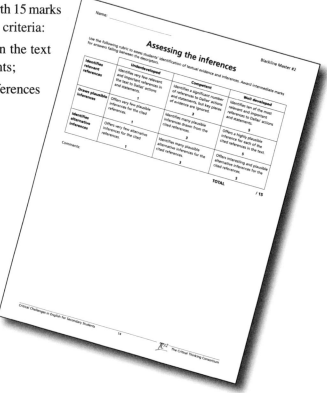

➤ Assess the position paper using *Assessing the paper* (Blackline Master #3). According to the rubric, the assignment is worth 20 marks and is evaluated on the following criteria:

- clearly expresses the student's position on the responsible characters;

- identifies the criteria used as the basis for the conclusion;

- offers ample evidence in relation to each criterion to support the conclusion;

- is technically proficient with complete sentences, cohesive paragraphs and proper spelling and punctuation.

Extension

➤ Ask students to write a short (1-2 pages) paper on one of the following topics:

- Is gallantry obsolete today? If so, why?

- Should gallantry survive as a desirable character trait?

- "Gallant" is often used to describe the actions of men. Explain how women's actions can also be considered gallant.

Reference

Hinton, S.E. (1995). *The Outsiders*. New York: Puffin Books.

Is Dallas gallant?

DALLAS' WORDS	PAGE	WHAT IT TELLS US ABOUT HIM	OTHER POSSIBLE INFERENCES
1. *"I'm never nice"*	22	Tries to appear "tough"	Low self-esteem
2.			
3.			
4.			
5.			
6.			
7.			
8.			
9.			
10.			
DALLAS' ACTIONS	PAGE	WHAT IT TELLS US ABOUT HIM	OTHER POSSIBLE INFERENCES
1. *Gives the boys money*	55	Shows he cares for his friends	Wants others to like him
2.			
3.			
4.			
5.			
6.			
7.			
8.			
9.			
10.			

Assessing the inferences

Use the following rubric to assess students' identification of textual evidence and inferences. Award intermediate marks for answers falling between the descriptors.

	Underdeveloped	**Competent**	**Well developed**
Identifies relevant references	Identifies very few relevant and important references in the text to Dallas' actions and statements. 1	Identifies a significant number of references to Dallas' actions and statements, but key pieces of evidence are ignored. 3	Identifies ten of the most relevant and important references to Dallas' actions and statements. 5
Draws plausible inferences	Offers very few plausible inferences for the cited references. 1	Identifies many plausible inferences drawn from the cited references. 3	Offers a highly plausible inference for each of the cited references in the text. 5
Identifies alternative inferences	Offers very few alternative inferences for the cited references. 1	Identifies many plausible alternative inferences for the cited references. 3	Offers interesting and plausible alternative inferences for the cited references. 5

TOTAL   **/ 15**

Comments:

Assessing the paper

Use the following rubric to assess students' position papers. Award intermediate marks for answers falling between the descriptors.

	Underdeveloped	**Competent**	**Well developed**
Clearly states a position	No clear position is expressed on the question asked. 1	Offers a position that only partly addresses the question asked. 3	Very clearly and succinctly expresses a position that directly addresses the question asked. 5
Identifies relevant criteria	Makes no obvious reference to the criteria used as the basis for reaching the conclusion. 1	Identifies some criteria for reaching the conclusion, but key factors are ignored. 3	Identifies all the key criteria used as the basis for reaching the conclusion. 5
Offers ample evidence	Offers no relevant evidence from the text. 1	Offers one piece of plausible evidence from the text for each criterion. 3	Offers three or more very plausible pieces of evidence from the text for each criterion. 5
Proficient at technical aspects	Writing may be ungrammatical, contain many spelling errors, and lack cohesive paragraphs and logical structure. 1	Writing is generally technically correct with well structured paragraphs, but may contain minor grammatical or spelling errors. 3	Writing is technically strong with correct grammar and accurate spelling, and cohesive, clear paragraphs. 5

Total   /20

Comments:

Who should we believe?

Critical Challenge

Critical question

Who provides a more believable picture of events in *The Pigman*, John or Lorraine?

Overview

In this challenge, students investigate the points of view of the two narrators in Paul Zindel's novel, *The Pigman,* to determine which narrator, John or Lorraine, provides a more credible account of events. The novel alternates between the two narrators, and as the point of view shifts, the reader is left wondering which character is more credible. Students complete a chart to analyze incidents reported differently by the narrators, and identify criteria for establishing the credibility of an account. The challenge concludes with a U-shaped discussion where students defend their assessment of the more reliable narrator.

Objectives

Broad understanding

Different perspectives on a single event can make it difficult to discover the truth.

Requisite tools

Background knowledge
- familiarity with the novel *The Pigman*

Criteria for judgment
- criteria for believability (e.g., consistency of information, plausibility of statement, credibility of character)

Critical thinking vocabulary
- point of view
- corroborating evidence
- conflicting evidence

Thinking strategies
- data chart

Habits of mind
- open-mindedness

Suggested Activities

Introduce point of view

➤ Show students two newspaper articles or letters to the editor on the same event or incident written from different points of view and discuss the differences between them. These items could be coverage of the same story from different newspapers or letters to the editor on the same issue from people with differing opinions.

point of view

Define point of view

➤ Ask students to work with a partner to formulate and write a definition of point of view. Share definitions in a class discussion and work towards a class definition of point of view.

Consider a local scenario

➤ Discuss a school event that could be seen from different points of view (for example, an incident that occurred in the cafeteria during lunch time as seen by the students involved, uninvolved observers, and the teachers or administrators supervising the cafeteria). Ask students to write a sentence or two about the incident from each point of view. Read some of these descriptions to the class and discuss the differences among the different points of view.

Determine credibility of accounts

➤ Introduce the following criteria for assessing the credibility of an account and work through an example on *What actually happened* (Blackline Master #1) before students begin this assignment individually or in pairs:

criteria for believability

• Is the account consistent with other information in the story?

• Is it plausible that things could have happened as stated?

• Does one character seem more credible than the other? If so, why?

Corroborate with evidence

➤ Invite students to assess the credibility of the two newspaper accounts with evidence from the text. Explain that corroborating evidence refers to statements or observations that back up or reinforce another statement. In a court of law, for example, accused persons may supply corroborating evidence (e.g., eyewitness accounts, photographs, police documents) that supports their account of what happened. Conflicting evidence is information that suggests that the event could not have happened as suggested by one of the persons.

corroborating evidence, conflicting evidence

Explore points of view in the novel

➤ If students have not already read *The Pigman*, assign this task. Introduce the differences between John and Lorraine's points of view. Remind students that the reader does not know whether what each character reports is true or accurate. Ask students to think about which of the two narrators offers the more credible version of the story as they read the novel.

Look for evidence

➤ Ask students to identify various incidents in the novel and to report John and Lorraine's account of each and to look for corroborating or conflicting evidence. Finally, ask students to offer their own interpretation of each event. Distribute one or more copies of *What actually happened?* (Blackline Master #1) for students to record their findings. After they are finished, briefly discuss some of the responses as a class.

Pose the critical question

➤ Pose the critical question:

Who provides a more believable picture of events in The Pigman, *John or Lorraine?*

Hold U-shaped discussion

➤ Arrange students in a U-shape and hold a discussion on the relative credibility of the two narrators. Ask students to seat themselves in the "U" according to their views on the two narrators: those who think John is clearly more believable on one side of the room, those who regard the narrators as equally believable are to take seats in the middle of the "U", and those who think Lorraine is clearly more believable would sit on the other end of the "U". During the discussion encourage students to explain their position and to move their seats to match any changes in their thinking in response to reasons offered by other students.

Prepare journal entry

➤ As a culminating activity ask students to prepare an entry in their journal on their final position on the credibility of John and Lorraine. Encourage students to provide evidence from the novel to support their position and also to include evidence from the text that might challenge their conclusion.

open-mindedness

Assess the data chart

➤ Assess *What actually happened?* (Blackline Master #1) using the rubric *Assessing the conflicting accounts* (Blackline Master #2). According to this rubric, this task is worth 15 marks, based on the following criteria:

- identifies John and Lorraine's accounts of each incident accurately and clearly;

- includes information from the text that corroborates or contradicts each account;

- offers a plausible account of what actually happened, given the evidence.

Assess the journal entry

➤ Assess students' final position on the issues using the rubric *Assessing the conclusion* (Blackline Master #3). According to this rubric the paper is worth 20 marks, based on the following criteria:

- states a clear position;

- provides evidence from the novel for the stated position;

- provides evidence from the novel that might challenge the stated position;

- offers a plausible conclusion given the evidence provided.

Extension

Write from a different viewpoint

➤ Write a description of an incident from the story from another point of view. For example, write about the party at Mr. Pignati's house from the policeman's point of view.

Reference

Zindel, Paul. (1983). *The Pigman*. New York: Bantam Books.

What actually happened?

As you locate evidence in the text to corroborate the accounts of each incident, look for consistency with other parts, plausibility of statements, and signs of who is the more credible character. Finally, offer what you think actually happened for each incident.

				Person A's statement about the incident
				Person B's statement about the incident
				Corroborating or conflicting evidence
				Your interpretation of what actually happened

Assessing the conflicting accounts

Use the following rubric to assess students' description and assessment of the conflicting accounts of the incidents. Award intermediate marks for answers falling between the descriptors.

	Underdeveloped	**Competent**	**Well developed**
Accurate reporting	The conflicting accounts of the incidents are not clearly and accurately reported. 1	The conflicting accounts of the incidents are generally clear and accurately reported, but key features are vague or missing. 3	The conflicting accounts of the incidents are very clearly and accurately reported. 5
Corroborating or conflicting evidence	Corroborating or conflicting evidence is not provided. 1	Corroborating or conflicting evidence is provided for half of the accounts. 3	Relevant corroborating or conflicting evidence for each of the accounts is provided. 5
Plausible personal interpretation	The personal interpretation offered for each incident is not plausible and not well-supported with evidence. 1	The personal interpretation offered for each incident is generally convincing and supported to some extent. 3	The personal interpretation offered for each incident is very plausible and well-supported with evidence. 5

TOTAL   **/ 15**

Comments:

Assessing the conclusion

Use the following rubric to assess students' justification of their conclusion. Award intermediate marks for answers falling between the descriptors.

	Underdeveloped	Competent	Well developed
Clearly states a position	The conclusion is unclear. 1	The conclusion is stated in general terms. 3	The conclusion is very clearly stated. 5
Identifies reasons for the conclusion	Identifies no relevant evidence from the text *for* the conclusion. 1	Identifies some relevant and important evidence from the text *for* the conclusion. 3	Identifies the most important evidence from the text *for* the conclusion. 5
Identifies reasons against the conclusion	Identifies no relevant evidence from the text *against* the conclusion. 1	Identifies some relevant and important evidence from the text *against* the conclusion. 3	Identifies the most important evidence from the text *against* the conclusion. 5
Offers plausible conclusion	The conclusion is implausible and not justifiable given the evidence provided. 1	The conclusion is plausible and somewhat justifiable in light of the evidence provided. 3	The conclusion is highly plausible and highly justifiable in light of the evidence provided. 5

Total **/20**

Comments:

Dumb blondes, stupid jocks and four-eyed nerds

Critical Challenge

Critical question

Create a poster which breaks down a stereotype for your assigned target group.

Overview

In this challenge, students explore the concept of stereotyping and develop strategies to break down stereotypes. The challenge is based on the novel *The Pigman* by Paul Zindel which contains many examples of stereotyping. After reading the novel, students brainstorm and discuss several examples of stereotyping found in *The Pigman*. They then look for stereotyping in the everyday world and the media. Finally, students work together to offer ways to dissolve stereotypes.

Objectives

Broad understanding

Stereotyping can be found everywhere and affects everyone, but we can choose to control it.

Requisite tools

Background knowledge
- familiarity with the novel *The Pigman*
- knowledge of anti-stereotyping strategies

Criteria for judgment
- features of an effective anti-stereotyping poster (e.g., presents a full portrait, has powerful impact, fairly represents the subject or group)

Critical thinking vocabulary
- stereotype

Thinking strategies
- role-play
- data chart

Habits of mind

Suggested Activities

Define stereotype

➤ Define the term "stereotype" using the following examples of stereotyping as a guideline. A stereotype can be:

- an unfair account of an *individual* where we focus on a narrow range of things about a person instead of the full picture. It is a stereotype because we fail to perceive the multiple features or attributes of an individual (for example, we may focus on the differences in a person's speech or skin colour but overlook a range of other ways in which she/he is very similar to us; or we focus on the times a person is grumpy while overlooking her/his sense of humour and willingness to help others);

- an unfair account of a *group* where we overgeneralize about the actions or features of a few members of that group. It is a stereotype because we fail to recognize the diversity within the group, and that all members of the group are not one particular way (that is, not all women are "soft," and not all convicts are mean).

Create a role-play

➤ To dramatize the fact that we often see things from different perspectives invite students to create a role-play based on the scenario below. Divide students into groups to develop a role-play in which several typical points of view are expressed.

role-play

The scenario: City planners building a skateboard park on a vacant lot in a residential area.

Role-play characters: police officer, parent, an elderly person, a teenager, a building contractor, a neighbour on the block where the park will be built, a manufacturer of skateboards.

Ask each group to select three or four characters whose views they will represent. Groups should develop and record their role-play script and provide instructions that capture tone or voice and facial expressions characteristic of this interest group (for example, anger, frustration, happiness, apprehension). Each group is to present their role-play to the class. Ask students to keep their scripts, because they will need them again for a later activity.

Debrief role-play

➤ After each presentation, debrief the scenario in a class discussion, using the following questions:

- What assumptions were made about how people would feel and act? Why?

- Do all people in a particular group fit the stereotype presented?

- Why might we feel the need to group, label or generalize about people?

Record observations

➤ As a homework assignment, ask students to examine two television shows or the ads in two magazines to observe stereotyping. They should record their observations on *Media stereotyping* (Blackline Master #1A & 1B). Direct students to focus on the portrayal of minority groups, people of colour, senior citizens, and teens.

Session Two

Blackline Master #2

Discuss observations

➤ As a class, discuss their observations of *Media stereotyping*. Elicit student feelings about the stereotypes, particularly those representing teens.

Assign groups

➤ Divide students into teams and assign each a community group about which there are commonly held stereotypes. The following list contains some suggestions for groups to assign: ethnic groups, religious groups, parents, teachers, teenagers, skaters, politicians police officers, homeless people, senior citizens. It may be useful to provide students with some examples of anti-stereotyping found in the media, for example, advertising that protrays men in primary care-giver roles or that includes a variety of ethnic groups, such as Benetton clothing ads.

List stereotypes

➤ Ask the student teams to list at least four commonly held stereotypes about their assigned community group. They should record the stereotypes on *Combatting stereotypes* (Blackline Master #2).

Brainstorm strategies to break down stereotypes

➤ Next, ask each team to brainstorm ways to defeat the identified stereotypes and record the four most effective strategies on *Combatting stereotypes*.

It might be useful to provide an example such as the following:

Target group: Teenagers

Stereotype: all teenagers shoplift (teens are greeted as they enter a store and followed until they make a purchase or leave the store)

Strategies for overcoming the stereotype:

- make eye-contact with merchant

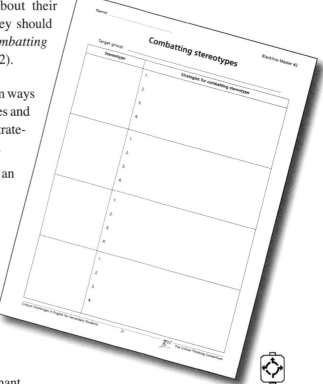

data chart

- greet them with a smile
- ask for help
- provide honest answers when employees ask if you need help.

Evaluate strategies

➤ Follow this activity with a brief group report and class discussion to evaluate strategies for overcoming stereotyping.

Session Three

Review role-play scripts

➤ Ask students to revisit their original role-play scripts and re-examine them in light of what they have learned about stereotyping by answering the following questions:

- Are the characters portrayed as stereotypes?
- To what degree are these fair or unfair portraits?
- What part of your role-play would you change?
- How might you do this?

knowledge of anti-stereotyping strategies

Revise scripts

➤ Ask students to rewrite the original script of their role-plays reflecting techniques they have learned by analyzing and brainstorming strategies for overcoming stereotyping.

Peer evaluation of scripts

➤ Direct teams to exchange both their original and adapted role-play scripts for peer evaluation with another team. Ask team members to provide feedback on the degree to which the adapted copy is free from stereotyping. Allow sufficient discussion time for this activity so students can add further suggestions about how to reduce stereotyped portraits to their role-play scripts.

Session Four

Create poster

➤ Present the critical task:

Create a poster which 'breaks down' a stereotype for your assigned target group.

Determine criteria

➤ Discuss with students criteria for making an effective anti-stereotyping poster. As a class make a list of the key features they should aim for in designing their poster (e.g., presents a full portrait of the group, has a powerful impact on the audience, fairly represents information).

features of effective anti-stereotyping posters

It may help students to begin with a profile of the stereotypes which exist for the particular group that is the subject of their poster. Encourage students to interview members of this target group to obtain a comprehensive image of them. Encourage students to collect images found in magazines or other visual sources. Depending on the extent of the research expected, allow one or two class sessions for students to complete their posters.

Assess media stereotyping

➤ Assess students' homework assignment, *Media stereotyping* using *Assessing "Media stereotyping"* (Blackline Master #3). According to this rubric, the assignment is worth 5 marks and is assessed on the clear identification and explanation of various examples of stereotyping.

Assess combatting stereotypes

➤ Assess *Combatting stereotypes* using *Assessing "Combatting stereotypes"* (Blackline Master #4). According to this rubric, the assignment is worth 10 marks and is assessed on two criteria:

- clearly identified examples of stereotyping;
- effective strategies to combat each of the four stereotypes.

Assess role-play scripts

➤ Assess the revised role-play scripts using *Assessing the role-play scripts* (Blackline Master #5). According to this rubric, the assignment is worth 5 marks and is assessed on the extent to which the revised scripts offer non-stereotypical positions taken by the characters portrayed.

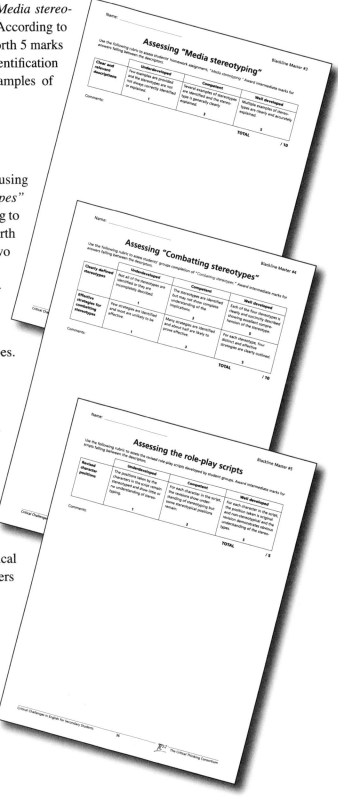

Assess the posters

➤ Assess the posters created by the students using *Assessing the posters* (Blackline Master #6). According to this rubric, the assignment is worth 10 marks and is assessed on two criteria:

• full and fair portrayal of the group;

• powerful impact on the audience.

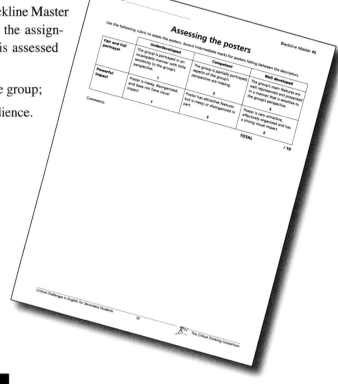

Extension

Combat media stereotyping

➤ Write a letter to a particular company or TV show identifying two or three examples of stereotyping in their advertising and suggesting how they could avoid stereotyping in their product ads. Mail the letters to the respective companies and wait for a response!

Continue with another challenge

➤ Follow this lesson with Critical Challenge E, "To Be or Not To Be," dealing with the reciprocal stereotyping that occurs between teenagers and seniors.

Extend to other stories

➤ Apply the activities in this lesson to other works of literature in which stereotyping is evident, for example, the short story "Charles" by Shirley Jackson.

Reference

Zindel, Paul. (1983). *The Pigman*. New York: Bantam Books.

Media stereotyping

	TELEVISION		
Program	**Example(s) of stereotyping**	**Source: program or ad**	**Time of day**
Friends	*Phoebe is the only blonde primary character and is portrayed as scattered and lacking seriousness. She is set up as a "dumb blonde" stereotype.*	*program*	*8:00 pm*

MAGAZINE		
Title of Magazine	**Advertisement**	**Example of Stereotyping**
Cosmopolitan	Calvin Klein	An extremely thin woman models for Calvin Klein. The stereotype is that to look good, women must be unnaturally thin.

Combatting stereotypes

Target group: _____

Stereotype	Strategies for combatting stereotype
	1. 2. 3. 4.
	1. 2. 3. 4.
	1. 2. 3. 4.
	1. 2. 3. 4.

Assessing "Media stereotyping"

Use the following rubric to assess students' homework assignment, "*Media stereotyping.*" Award intermediate marks for answers falling between the descriptors.

	Underdeveloped	Competent	Well developed
Clear and relevant descriptions	Few examples are provided and the stereotypes are not not always correctly identified or explained. 1	Several examples of stereotypes are identified and the stereotype is generally clearly explained. 3	Multiple examples of stereotypes are clearly and accurately explained. 5

TOTAL   **/ 10**

Comments:

Assessing "Combatting stereotypes"

Use the following rubric to assess students' groups completion of "*Combatting stereotypes.*" Award intermediate marks for answers falling between the descriptors.

	Underdeveloped	Competent	Well developed
Clearly defined stereotypes	Not all of the stereotypes are identified or they are incompletely described. **1**	The stereotypes are identified but may not show complete understanding of the implications. **3**	Each of the four stereotypes is clearly and succinctly described showing excellent comprehension of the stereotype. **5**
Effective strategies for combatting stereotypes	Few strategies are identified and most are unlikely to be effective. **1**	Many strategies are identified and about half are likely to prove effective. **3**	For each stereotype, four distinct and effective strategies are clearly outlined. **5**

TOTAL **/ 10**

Comments:

Assessing the role-play scripts

Use the following rubric to assess the revised role-play scripts developed by student groups. Award intermediate marks for scripts falling between the descriptors.

	Underdeveloped	**Competent**	**Well developed**
Revised character positions	The positions taken by the characters in the script remain stereotyped and show little or no understanding of stereotyping.	For each character in the script, the revisions show understanding of stereotyping but some stereotypical positions remain.	For each character in the script, the position taken is original and non-stereotypical and the revision demonstrates obvious understanding of the stereotypes.
	1	**3**	**5**

TOTAL   **/ 5**

Comments:

Assessing the posters

Use the following rubric to assess the posters. Award intermediate marks for posters falling between the descriptors.

	Underdeveloped	Competent	Well developed
Fair and full portrayal	The group is portrayed in an incomplete manner with little sensitivity to the group's perspective. **1**	The group is partially portrayed; aspects of the group's perspective are missing. **3**	The group's main features are well represented and presented in a manner that is sensitive to the group's perspective. **5**
Powerful impact	Poster is messy, disorganized, and does not have visual impact. **1**	Poster has attractive features but is messy or disorganized in part. **3**	Poster is very attractive, effectively organized and has a strong visual impact. **5**

TOTAL   **/ 10**

Comments:

To be or not to be

Critical task

Design a questionnaire, using a set of probing questions, to investigate seniors' attitudes towards teenagers.

Overview

In this challenge, students investigate stereotyping by researching senior citizens' attttudes towards teenagers (or some other group that is often stereotyped by teenagers). Students begin by exploring their own pre-conceptions about seniors (or another group) and question whether or not their perceptions are based on stereotypes. Students next learn to ask probing questions leading to the design of a questionnaire to uncover how teenagers are actually perceived by local senior citizens, what teenagers do to create these perceptions and what they might do to counter them. Finally students redesign the questionnaire with an eye to making the questions more probing. As a by-product of preparing the questionnaire and analyzing the results, students confront their own stereotypical assumptions about elderly people.

This lesson links thematically with *The Pigman* by Paul Zindel, and can be used as a follow-up to the critical challenge on stereotyping, "Dumb Blondes, Stupid Jocks and Four-Eyed Nerds" (Critical Challenge D).

Objectives

Broad understanding

Stereotypes can be broken down when we seek to understand other perspectives.

Requisite tools

Background knowledge
- knowledge of seniors' attitudes towards teenagers

Criteria for judgment
- criteria for identifying a probing question (e.g., clearly stated, open-ended, seeks specific information)

Critical thinking vocabulary
- stereotype

Thinking strategies

Habits of mind
- open-mindedness

Suggested Activities

Record initial thoughts

➤ Distribute *Thinking about seniors* (Blackline Master #1) and ask students to write in the "First Thoughts" column their answers to the following questions:

- What is your attitude towards seniors?
- What is their attitude towards you?
- What behaviour do you display when you are around seniors?
- How do you feel when seniors generalize about teenagers?

Explore ideas about seniors

➤ Divide the board into three sections. Write the phrase "senior citizens" (or another group's name) in the middle of the board and, without explanation, ask students to list any associations they have regarding this group on a piece of paper. Ask students to share their ideas in an open class discussion. Record students' ideas on the board in a web around the phrase "senior citizen." (If the discussion is slow to get started, ask students what they think seniors' attitudes towards teenagers are.)

Question perceptions

➤ Referring to the ideas about seniors recorded on the board, ask the class "Why do we believe these to be true?" Compile students' responses by writing them on a second section of the board.

Define "stereotype"

➤ Define the term "stereotype" or review the definition of stereotype from the critical challenge, "Dumb Blondes, Stupid Jocks and Four Eyed Nerds" (page 24).

stereotype

Identify stereotypes

➤ On the third section of the board, record students' responses to the following questions:

- Are all seniors actually like this or are these stereotypes?
- What information would we need to confirm our views?

As a class, reflect on the ideas recorded on the board.

Revisit "first thoughts"

➤ Ask students to revisit they recorded on *Thinking about seniors* in the "First Thoughts" column and highlight any stereotypical statements. Ask students to explain *why* these highlighted comments are stereotypical in the "Second Thoughts" column. Divide students into small groups (3-5 students each) to assess each other's work, checking whether or not each individual has recognized and adequately explained his/her stereotypes.

open-mindedness

Session Two

Develop criteria for a questionnaire

➤ Suggest that the class find out exactly what perceptions seniors have of teenagers and why they have these perceptions. Discuss creating a questionnaire. Explain that students must generate thoughtful, probing questions that effectively get to the root of the issue. Invite students to offer criteria to identify good probing questions. Below are suggestions that students might consider:

A probing question . . .
- is clearly worded;
- is open-ended (as opposed to closed-ended);
- is respectful of the person responding;
- makes no accusations or unfounded assumptions;
- seeks specific information.

criteria for probing questions

Examine poorly-worded questions

➤ Provide students with a few examples of flawed questions (e.g., Why do you guys hassle us so often? What is your problem?) and ask students to apply the criteria to these questions. Confirm that each student understands what is implied by the criteria and that the list of criteria they have developed is adequate. Agree on a list of criteria for identifying a thoughtful, probing question and post this list in a prominent place in the classroom.

Begin writing questions

➤ Invite each student to write down two probing questions he or she would like to ask of senior citizens to uncover their attitudes towards teenagers. Remind students to produce questions that meet the criteria for probing questions. Tell students their questions will be assessed according to these criteria.

Evaluate questions in small groups

➤ Arrange students in small groups to share and evaluate their questions in light of the agreed-upon criteria. If warranted, students should revise their questions so that they better meet the criteria. Instruct each group to write a set of up to 10 probing questions on an overhead.

Evaluate questions as a class

➤ Using an overhead projector, consider as a class each group's questions and evaluate them in light of the criteria. If questions are redundant or overlap, choose the better question or consolidate the questions. Record on the board the emerging list of recommended questions.

Rank questions

➤ Ask students working in small groups to rank order the questions according to their effectiveness in serving the purpose of the questionnaire, to find out what seniors actually think about teenagers and why they think as they do. As a class decide on a suitable number of questions, perhaps from 7 to 12 questions in total and select the top recommendations from the ranked lists.

Session Three   *Blackline Master #2*

Prepare questionnaire

➤ Using the questions developed by the class, create a draft questionnaire and distribute it for final review by students. Add or delete questions as students see collectively fit and prepare the final copy of the questionnaire. See *Information survey* (Blackline Master #2) for an actual questionnaire developed by a grade 9 class.

Distribute questionnaire

➤ Distribute the final questionnaire to a sample of approximately 20 senior citizens, either by contacting a local senior's centre or by having students approach seniors they know who will distribute the questionnaire to fellow seniors. If possible, arrange a field trip where students can meet seniors and distribute th questionnaire. Arrange for the completed questionnaires to be returned directly to the school as soon as possible.

Review completed questionnaire

➤ When a sufficient number of completed questionnaires have been returned, make copies for each group of 3-5 students. Ask student groups to review the completed questionnaires with two purposes in mind: to learn more about how seniors actually feel about teenagers and to use the responses from the completed questionnaires to improve the questions asked on the questionnaire.

seniors' attitudes towards teenagers

The small student groups should read over the questionnaire responses and then discuss the following questions:

• What were you surprised to learn about senior's perceptions?

• Were any of your preconceptions about the views of seniors unfounded?

• What have you learned about your role/place in this community and in society more generally?

• What have you learned about stereotyping others and about how to avoid being stereotyped yourself?

Discuss reactions as a class

➤ In a class discussion, invite students to share their reactions to the seniors' responses. Focus students' attention on the stereotypes that they may have held about seniors.

➤ Ask students to again revisit *Thinking about seniors* (Blackline Master #1) and complete the column "Third Thoughts" by reviewing what they wrote in the other two columns and heard in the class discussions. Students should write any final thoughts or comments about how their thinking has changed or deepened.

open-mindedness

Session Four   *Blackline Master #3*

Introduce the critical task

➤ Use any confusion or uncertainty arising from students' interpretations of questionnaire responses to raise the possibility of obtaining more and better information from seniors. Ask "could we have developed a more probing set of questions?" Present the critical task:

> *Design a questionnaire, using a set of probing questions, to investigate seniors' attitudes towards teenagers.*

Revise the questions

➤ Ask students to create their own revised questionnaire. It may be helpful to provide students with a response format such as the one outlined in *Improving the questionnaire* (Blackline Master #3). Students are to revise the original questionnaire based on the responses received. Suggest that students ask themselves the following questions as they think about each question:

- Do the responses match the intention of the question?

- How might it be improved (i.e., be made more probing)?

- Should the question be deleted?

- What additional question, if any, would be useful to ask?

Students may wish to revise or add to the previously developed list of criteria for probing questions.

Assess the initial questions

➤ Assess the two questions posed initially by the students using the rubric *Assessing the quetions* (Blackline Master #4). According to this rubric the assignment is worth 15 marks and is assessed on three criteria:

- questions are clear and concise;
- questions seek specific and relevant information;
- questions are open-ended.

Assess revised questionnaire

➤ Assess students' revised questionnaires recorded on *Improving the questionnaire* (Blackline Master #5). According to this rubric, the assignment is worth 10 marks and is assessed on two criteria:

- amount of improvement;
- addresses criteria for a probing question.

Extension

Consider value of revision

➤ A recurring theme in this critical challenge is the differences that occur when we revisit initial ideas after gathering additional information. What differences have students noticed in the before and after? Do they find this process of revisiting useful? worth the effort?

Survey additional seniors

➤ Suggest that students send out their revised questionnaires to a new group of seniors to see what additional insights they can gain about seniors' attitudes towards teenagers.

Combat misconceptions

➤ Invite students to decide upon and implement a strategy (or set of strategies) to improve perceptions between seniors and teenagers. This activity ties in with the critical challenge "Dumb Blondes, Stupid Jocks and Four-Eyed Nerds" (Critical Challenge D).

Reference

Zindel, Paul. (1983). *The Pigman*. New York: Bantam Books.

Thinking about seniors

FIRST THOUGHTS	SECOND THOUGHTS	FINAL THOUGHTS
What is your attitude towards seniors?		
What is their attitude towards you?		
What behaviour do you display when you are around seniors?		
How do you feel when you hear seniors generalizing about teenagers?		

Information survey

The students of Ms. Shea's English 9 class are studying a novel that deals with the relationship between two teenagers and an older man. They have put together the following survey in the hopes of gaining a better understanding of how they are perceived by seniors in their community and what they do to promote these perceptions.

Please answer each question as fully as possible. Be honest!

1. How do you feel when other people criticize teenagers? Do you tend to join in or defend the teens? Why?

2. What is the first thought that comes into your mind when you see a group of teenagers? What makes you think this?

3. What do you think teens should do to be seen more positively in the eyes of the community?

4. What would you like to know about teenagers and their lifestyle?

5. What do you think about teenagers' appearance (dress, hair styles, etc.)?

6. Do you think that you have ever prejudged teenagers based on stereotypes? Explain your reasoning.

7. Explain how you feel about the actions of teenagers in general. How do these actions affect you?

8. Why do you think some people have a negative attitude towards teens today?

9. How is a teenager today different from when you were a teenager?

10. What would you change about teenagers today if you had the power to do so?

11. If a rock hit your window and broke it and you looked outside and saw a neatly dressed teen and a teen wearing baggy clothes, who would you be more likely to suspect and why?

Example of a questionnaire prepared by Nancy Shea's grade 9 English class at Southern Okanagan Secondary in Oliver, B.C.

Improving the questionnaire

Instructions: You have been asked to suggest how the class-designed questionnaire could be improved. In the column on the left, beneath each of the original questions asked on our questionnaire, indicate what improvements, if any, (including replacing the question completely) you would recommend. In the column on the right justify each of your suggestions by explaining how your changes make the question more powerful.

QUESTION	REASON FOR CHANGE
Original question: 1. *Suggested revision:*	
Original question: 2. *Suggested revision:*	
Original question: 3. *Suggested revision:*	
Original question: 4. *Suggested revision:*	

QUESTION	REASON FOR CHANGE
Original question: 5. *Suggested revision:*	
Original question: 6. *Suggested revision:*	
Original question: 7. *Suggested revision:*	
Original question: 8. *Suggested revision:*	
Original question: 9. *Suggested revision:*	
Original question: 10. *Suggested revision:*	

Assessing the questions

Use the following rubric to assess students' two questions. Award intermediate marks for answers falling between the descriptors.

	Underdeveloped	**Competent**	**Well developed**
Clear and concise questions	Neither question is clearly posed nor concisely stated. 1	One questions is clear and concise but the other needs improvement. 3	Both questions are clearly and succinctly posed. 5
Specific and relevant questions	Neither question asks for specific, relevant information but instead are vaguely worded. 1	Only one of the questions seeks specific, relevant information. 3	Both questions target specific, relevant information. 5
Open-ended questions	Both questions are closed and can be ans wered with "yes" or "no". 1	Only one question is open-ended and the other is closed. 3	Both questions are open-ended. 5

TOTAL / 15

Comments:

Assessing the questionnaires

Use the following rubric to assess the revised questionnaires on *Improving the questionnaire* (Blackline Master #3). Award intermediate marks for answers falling between the descriptors.

	Underdeveloped	**Competent**	**Well developed**
Amount of improvement	Very few revisions are suggested and often they do not improve the questions. 1	A number of revisions are suggested which improve the questions to some extent. 3	Where ever possible the revisions significantly improve the questions. 5
Address criteria for probing questions	The revised set of questions are still flawed in many respects. 1	Many questions meet the criteria for probing questions to some extent. 3	All of the questions clearly meet the criteria for probing questions. 5

TOTAL   **/ 10**

Comments:

Should it stay or go?

Critical Challenge

Critical task

A. Assess the appropriateness of the selected piece of literature for inclusion in the curriculum.

B. Write a letter to the provincial Ministry of Education arguing for or against the inclusion of the piece of literature in the curriculum.

Overview

Every teacher has been faced with the question: "Why are we studying this novel?" This challenge invites students to work through this question. *My Left Foot,* by Christy Brown, a novel suitable for senior high students, is used as an example, but this approach could be adapted to evaluate any novel at any grade level. Students determine criteria for selecting curriculum resources and then test a novel against these criteria, defending their position in a formal letter to the provincial Ministry of Education.

Objectives

Broad understanding

There are specific criteria that can be used to evaluate whether a novel or story is appropriate for study in school.

Requisite tools

Background knowledge

- familiarity with *My Left Foot* or other literature selection

Criteria for judgment

- qualities of a novel or story appropriate for use in schools (e.g., interest to audience, rich use of language, universal message, appropriateness to audience)

- qualities of a well-written persuasive letter (e.g., explains criteria for assessment, provides detailed support, written in proper format)

Critical thinking vocabulary

Thinking strategies

- rating scale

Habits of mind

- open-mindedness

Suggested Activities

Identify favoured books

➤ As part of the closing activities after a short story or novel study (in this case, Christy Brown's *My Left Foot*), students will develop arguments in defense of its place in the provincial curriculum. Introduce the lesson by asking students the following questions and recording their responses on the board:

familiarity with the novel

- What is your favourite book/story among those you have read for school? Your least favourite?

- What is your "all time" favourite book/story?

Determine attributes of a good book

➤ Once students have collectively listed their favourite books, divide students into small groups that will compile a list of the attributes of a good book. This is best done on chart paper so that the lists can be displayed for comparison among groups.

qualities of an appropriate novel

After all the groups' charts have been displayed, discuss the common criteria of a good book and reduce this list to approximately five criteria. Some criteria may include:

- interesting to audience;

- contains rich use of language;

- has a universal message (an important message with broad appeal).

Explore educational criteria

➤ Invite students to discuss whether a novel used in school requires that any additional criteria be met. Write students' ideas on the board.

Explain how curriculum resources are selected in your province, focussing on the criteria that students believe ought to be established by the Ministry of Education for including a book in the curriculum. Introduce social dimensions that ministries consider, such as gender equity, political or ethnic biases, portrayal of violence and language use. Encourage students to re-assess their criteria for a good book in light of the considerations that govern provincial selection of reading materials.

Evaluate the novel

➤ Divide students into small groups and distribute copies of *Curriculum resource selection* (Blackline Master #1) for the groups to complete, adding two criteria they consider useful for resource selection. It may be helpful to begin this activity as a class, completing the first criterion as follows:

Key features of a good novel	Looks like? Sounds like?	Example from novel
Interesting to audience very weak fair satisfactory good excellent **1** **2** **3** (**3.5**)**4** **5**	*Looks like a book you can't put down*	*Pregnant mom falls down stairs while caring for her disabled son; disabled son has to get help for the mom*

rating scale

Discuss the first critical challenge

➤ After groups have used Blackline Master #1 to evaluate the novel, invite the class to discuss whether or not this novel should be a recommended resource. Present the critical task:

> *Assess the appropriateness of the selected piece of literature for inclusion in the curriculum.*

Coach students to develop arguments for or against its inclusion in the curriculum. Remind students to make explicit references to the criteria for selection when offering reasons for their position.

Session Two   *Blackline Master #2*

Introduce the second critical task

➤ Once students are confident in their arguments and have generated sufficient criteria to support their positions, introduce the letter writing assignment and discuss the importance of audience when writing and developing arguments. Present the critical task:

> *Write a letter to the provincial Ministry of Education arguing for or against the inclusion of the piece of literature in the curriculum.*

qualities of a formal letter

Provide letter format

➤ Make a transparency of *Formal letter template* (Blackline Master #2) to show students the format of a formal persuasive letter on an overhead projector. Discuss the following evaluation criteria to assist students in drafting this letter:

- a clear explanation of criteria is used for judging curriculum selection;

- appropriate, specific examples from the novel are cited to support the conclusion reached;

- a polite tone is used;

- the letter is error-free (i.e., spelling, grammar and style).

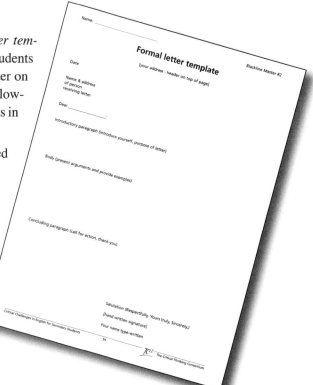

The Critical Thinking Consortium

Assess the rating

➤ Assess students' evaluation as recorded on *Curriculum resource selection* (Blackline Master #1) using the rubric *Assessing the rating* (Blackline Master #3). According to this rubric, the assignment is worth 10 marks and is assessed on two criteria:

- includes relevant evidence for each attribute of a good novel;
- evidence supports the assigned ratings.

Assess the formal letter

➤ Assess students' letters using *Formal letter evaluation* (Blackline Master #4). Assessment may be conducted by peers, the teacher or both. According to this rubric, the assignment is worth 20 marks and is assessed on four criteria:

- the criteria for evaluating resources are clearly identified;
- appropriate supporting examples are cited;
- letters are technically proficient and free of grammar and spelling errors;
- the tone is polite and respectful.

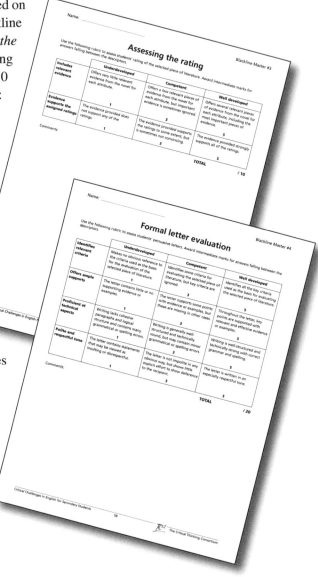

Extension

Consult Ministry criteria

➤ Obtain a copy of the provincial resource selection criteria from the Ministry of Education and ask students to compare their criteria to the provincially-approved criteria.

Reference

Brown, Christy. (1995). *My Left Foot*. London: Mandarin Paperbacks.

Curriculum resource selection

Novel title: _____

Key features of a good novel	Looks like? Sounds like?	Examples from text
Interesting to audience very fair satisfactory good excellent weak 1 2 3 4 5		
Rich use of language very fair satisfactory good excellent weak 1 2 3 4 5		
Important universal message very fair satisfactory good excellent weak 1 2 3 4 5		
Appropriateness to general audience/age of audience very fair satisfactory good excellent weak 1 2 3 4 5		
  very fair satisfactory good excellent weak 1 2 3 4 5		
  very fair satisfactory good excellent weak 1 2 3 4 5		

Formal letter template

[your address - header on top of page]

Date

Name & address
of person
receiving letter

Dear _____:

Introductory paragraph (introduce yourself, purpose of letter)

Body (present arguments and provide examples)

Concluding paragraph (call for action, thank-you)

Salutation (Respectfully, Yours truly, Sincerely,)

[hand written signature]

Your name type-written

Assessing the rating

Use the following rubric to assess students' rating of the selected piece of literature. Award intermediate marks for answers falling between the descriptors.

	Underdeveloped	**Competent**	**Well developed**
Includes relevant evidence	Offers very little relevant evidence from the novel for each attribute. 1	Offers a few relevant pieces of evidence from the novel for each attribute, but important evidence is sometimes ignored. 3	Offers several relevant pieces of evidence from the novel for each attribute, including the most important pieces of evidence. 5
Evidence supports the assigned ratings	The evidence provided does not support any of the ratings. 1	The evidence provided supports the ratings to some extent, but is sometimes not convincing. 3	The evidence provided strongly supports all of the ratings. 5

TOTAL   **/ 10**

Comments:

Formal letter evaluation

Use the following rubric to assess students' persuasive letters. Award intermediate marks for answers falling between the descriptors.

	Underdeveloped	**Competent**	**Well developed**
Identifies relevant criteria	Makes no obvious reference to the criteria used as the basis for the evaluation of the selected piece of literature. 1	Identifies some criteria for evaluating the selected piece of literature, but key criteria are ignored. 3	Identifies all the key criteria used as the basis for evaluating the selected piece of literature. 5
Offers ample supports	The letter contains little or no supporting evidence or examples. 1	The letter supports some points with evidence or examples, but these are missing in other cases. 3	Throughout the letter, key points are supported with relevant and effective evidence or examples. 5
Proficient at technical aspects	Writing lacks cohesive paragraphs and logical structure and contains many grammatical or spelling errors. 1	Writing is generally well-structured and technically sound, but may contain minor grammatical or spelling errors. 3	Writing is well-structured and technically strong with correct grammar and spelling. 5
Polite and respectful tone	The letter contains statements that may be viewed as insulting or disrespectful. 1	The letter is not impolite in any obvious way, but shows little explicit effort to show deference to the recipient. 3	The letter is written in an especially respectful tone. 5

TOTAL   **/ 20**

Comments:

Like a rolling stone

Critical Challenge

Critical question

Should Jack, Ralph or Roger be charged with homicide under the Criminal Code for the death of Piggy?

Overview

In this challenge, students must decide whether or not Jack, Ralph or Roger, characters in the novel *Lord of the Flies* by William Golding, deserve to be charged with a homicide offense. This novel offers a scathing look at human nature and society. In it, a physically unappealing character named Piggy is killed by a group of boys who have become uncivilized. Students review the legal definitions of the terms manslaughter, first degree murder and second degree murder, and collect evidence from the novel to determine whether Jack, Ralph or Roger should be charged with a homicide offense, and if so, which offense.

Objectives

Broad understanding

The legal culpability for a homicide offence depends on whether the evidence suggests that the person's actions meet the required criteria.

Requisite tools

Background knowledge
- familiarity with the novel *The Lord of the Flies*
- familiarity with the terms "first degree murder," "second degree murder" and "manslaughter"

Criteria for judgment
- criteria for determining guilt for each of the homicide offenses (e.g., deliberate act, mitigating circumstances, unforeseen events)

Critical thinking vocabulary
- manslaughter
- first and second degree murder

Thinking strategies
- data chart
- pro and con evidence

Habits of mind

Suggested Activities

Introduce key legal terms

➤ Ask students if they know how the terms "murder" and "manslaughter" are defined in the Criminal Code. Divide students into small groups to discuss the meaning of these terms, and to record their definitions. Invite a member from each group to read out their definitions of these terms.

familiarity with the types of homicide

Explore criteria for each offense

➤ Distribute copies of *Conditions for homicide* (Blackline Master #1). As a class, look at the Criminal Code definitions. Point out the fundamental difference between murder and manslaughter:

the conditions for types of homicide

- murder: The unlawful killing of a person with malice—i.e., the active deliberate intention of committing an unlawful action.

- manslaughter: The unlawful killing of a person without malice.

Review Criminal Code definitions

➤ Review the distinctions between murder in the *first degree*—deliberate killing with certain accompanying conditions (i.e., the victim was a police officer, the murder took place during a kidnapping) and murder in the *second degree*—deliberate killing where the accompanying conditions are not present. Point out that a charge is laid against a person only if there seems to be sufficient evidence that the crime has been committed by that person.

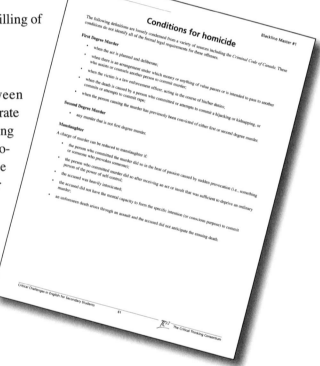

Collect evidence from the novel

➤ Ask students to collect evidence from the novel that could be used to justify a homicide charge against Jack, Ralph or Roger. Students may work individually or they could be divided into groups in which individual students are assigned certain chapters to read. This task may be assigned as homework or an extra session may be scheduled so students can complete their research in class.

familiarity with the novel

Explain data chart

➤ Suggest that students use *Evidence for homicide* (Blackline Master #2) to record the information found about each character and to indicate which, if any, charge the collected evidence suggests is justifiable.

data chart

Session Two

Present the critical question

➤ Present the critical question:

Should Jack, Ralph or Roger be charged with homicide under the Criminal Code for the death of Piggy?

Prepare their recommendations

➤ Ask students to write a two-page essay in which they argue whether there is enough evidence to charge any of the boys with a homicide offense, and which, if any, charge is suggested by the evidence they have collected. Encourage students to consider the evidence that exists for the charges they would recommend and to consider possible evidence (or incomplete evidence) that might raise doubts about their recommendations.

Assess data charts

➤ Assess students' data charts using *Assessing "Evidence for homicide"* (Blackline Master #3). According to this rubric, the assignment is worth 10 marks and is assessed on two criteria:

- amount of relevant evidence recorded;
- plausible selection of the appropriate charge for each character.

Assess the recommended charges

➤ Assess the essays using *Assessing the recommended charges* (Blackline Master #4). According to this rubric, the assignment is worth 20 marks and is assessed on four criteria:

- precisely states charges;
- identifies evidence for the recommended charges;
- identifies evidence against the recommended charges;
- the recommended charges are plausible in light of the evidence provided.

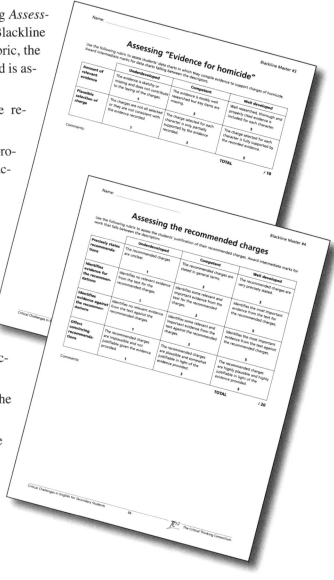

Extension

Role-play one of the lawyers

➤ Invite students to take on the role of either defense counsel or Crown counsel and develop a case that they would present at the trial of either Jack, Ralph or Roger.

Carry out a mock trial

➤ Conduct a mock trial based on the evidence collected in this activity. Discuss with students the burden of proof required to establish guilt in criminal cases, namely that the person must be guilty beyond a reasonable doubt (i.e., any doubts about innocence must be based on reasons and not simply be imagined doubts).

Reference

Golding, William. (1954) *Lord of the Flies*. London: Faber & Faber.

Conditions for homicide

The following definitions are loosely condensed from a variety of sources including the *Criminal Code of Canada*. These conditions do not identify all of the formal legal requirements for these offenses.

First Degree Murder

- when the act is planned and deliberate;

- when there is an arrangement under which money or anything of value passes or is intended to pass to another who assists or counsels another person to commit murder;

- when the victim is a law enforcement officer, acting in the course of his/her duties;

- when the death is caused by a person who committed or attempts to commit a hijacking or kidnapping, or commits or attempts to commit rape;

- when the person causing the murder has previously been convicted of either first or second degree murder.

Second Degree Murder

- any murder that is not first degree murder.

Manslaughter

A charge of murder can be reduced to manslaughter if:

- the person who committed the murder did so in the heat of passion caused by sudden provocation (i.e., something or someone who provokes someone);

- the person who committed murder did so after receiving an act or insult that was sufficient to deprive an ordinary person of the power of self-control;

- the accused was heavily intoxicated;

- the accused did not have the mental capacity to form the specific intention (or conscious purpose) to commit murder;

- an unforeseen death arises through an assault and the accused did not anticipate the ensuing death.

Evidence for homicide

Conditions for homicide	Jack	Ralph	Roger
First degree murder			
• planned and deliberate			
• money or valuables given			
• victim is law enforcement officer			
• involves hijacking, kidnapping or rape			
• was previously convicted of murder			
Reduced to manslaughter			
• heat of passion			
• over-powering insult			
• heavily intoxicated			
• mental incapacity			
• unforeseen death			

Which, if any, charge is most appropriate? _____ _____ _____

Assessing "Evidence for homicide"

Use the following rubric to assess students' data charts in which they compile evidence to support charges of homicide. Award intermediate marks for data charts falling between the descriptors.

	Underdeveloped	**Competent**	**Well developed**
Amount of relevant evidence	The evidence is sketchy or missing and does not contribute to the laying of the charges. 1	The evidence is mostly well researched but key items are missing. 3	Well researched, thorough and properly cited evidence is included for each character. 5
Plausible selection of charge	The charges are not all selected or they are not consistent with the evidence recorded. 1	The charge selected for each character is only partially supported by the evidence recorded. 3	The charge selected for each character is fully supported by the recorded evidence. 5

TOTAL **/ 10**

Comments:

Assessing the recommended charges

Use the following rubric to assess the students' justification of their recommended charges. Award intermediate marks for work that falls between the descriptors.

	Underdeveloped	**Competent**	**Well developed**
Precisely states recommenda-tions	The recommended charges are unclear. 1	The recommended charges are stated in general terms. 3	The recommended charges are very precisely stated. 5
Identifies evidence for the recommen-dations	Identifies no relevant evidence from the text *for* the recommended charges. 1	Identifies some relevant and important evidence from the text *for* the recommended charges. 3	Identifies the most important evidence from the text *for* the recommended charges. 5
Identifies evidence against the recommen-dations	Identifies no relevant evidence from the text *against* the recommended charges. 1	Identifies some relevant and important evidence from the text *against* the recommended charges. 3	Identifies the most important evidence from the text *against* the recommended charges. 5
Offers convincing recommenda-tions	The recommended charges are implausible and not justifiable given the evidence provided. 1	The recommended charges are plausible and somewhat justifiable in light of the evidence provided. 3	The recommended charges are highly plausible and highly justifiable in light of the evidence provided. 5

TOTAL   / 20

Comments:

Leader of the pack

Critical Challenge

Critical question

Which character in *Lord of the Flies* has stronger leadership qualities, Jack or Ralph?

Overview

This is the first of two challenges that use William Golding's novel *Lord of the Flies* as a springboard from which to investigate leadership qualities. In this challenge, students explore the attributes of good leaders and assess whether two main characters in the novel, Ralph and Jack, possess these attributes. Students then judge which of these characters has the stronger leadership qualities.

Objectives

Broad understanding

Strong leaders may possess differing characters traits and personal qualities.

Requisite tools

Background knowledge
- familiarity with the novel *The Lord of the Flies*

Criteria for judgment
- attributes of strong leadership (e.g., honesty, respect for others, determination)

Critical thinking vocabulary

Thinking strategies
- data chart
- rating scale

Habits of mind
- open-mindedness

Suggested Activities

Introduce leadership qualities

➤ To help students begin thinking about the qualities that characterize strong leaders, ask members of the class to name several individuals they judge to be good leaders. Record these names in a column on the board.

data chart

Develop criteria for strong leadership

➤ Divide students into small groups to consider the attributes possessed by these and other leaders. Distribute *Leadership profiles* (Blackline Master #1) and invite students to identify and list two leaders at each of the school, community and national/international levels. For each leader, students should discuss and record one or two attributes that make this person stand out as a leader. Point out the example of Martin Luther King, Jr. included on the blackline master.

Select important leadership qualities

➤ Once completed, ask students to share information from their data charts in a class discussion. List the attributes of good leadership that students identify in a second column on the board. On the basis of the class discussion, invite students to select the five most important leadership attributes.

attributes of good leadership

Record evidence

➤ Distribute a copy of *Jack's and Ralph's leadership* (Blackline Master #2) to each student. Ask students to copy the list of the five most important leadership attributes into the left-hand column on the data chart.

Look for evidence

➤ Direct students to consult the novel looking for evidence that suggests whether or not Jack and Ralph possess these attributes. Students should record this evidence in the appropriate columns on the data chart. Invite students to share their findings with other members of their group. On the basis of the evidence, each student is to rate on a scale of 1 to 3 the degree to which Jack and Ralph exhibit each of the agreed-upon attributes.

rating scale

Ask the critical question

➤ Once each student has completed Blackline Master #2, present the critical question:

> *Which character in Lord of the Flies has stronger leadership qualities, Jack or Ralph?*

Conduct discussion

➤ Arrange students in a U-shape and hold a classroom discussion to determine which of the two main characters possesses the stronger leadership qualities. Ask students to seat themselves in the "U" according to the position they take about the stronger leader: those who think Jack is obviously the better leader sit at the top end of the U on one side of the room, those who see the characters as equally strong leaders are to take seats in the middle of the U, and those who think Ralph is clearly the stronger leader are to sit on the other end of the U.

Justify choice

➤ During the discussion encourage students to clarify their position and to offer reasons from the novel to support their views. Provide several opportunities for students to move their seats to match any changes in their position on the respective strength of the two leaders.

open-mindedness

Prepare journal entry

➤ As a culminating activity ask students to choose whether Jack or Ralph is the character with the stronger leadership qualities and write a journal entry justifying this position. Encourage students to provide evidence from the novel that might challenge their conclusion in addition to providing the evidence to support their position.

Evaluation ▸ *Blackline Masters #3-4*

Assess the rating of attributes

➤ Assess students' evaluation of each character's leadership qualities as recorded on *Jack's and Ralph's leadership* (Blackline Master #2) using the rubric *Assessing the ratings* (Blackline Master #3). According to this rubric, the assignment is worth 10 marks and is assessed on two criteria:

• includes relevant evidence for each leadership attribute;

• evidence supports the assigned ratings.

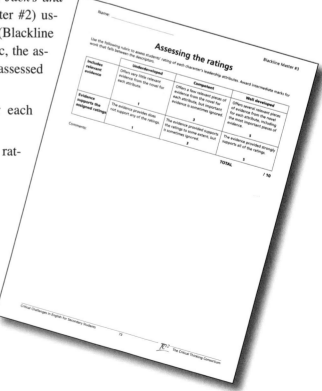

➤ Assess students' journal entries using *Assessing the conclusion* (Blackline Master #3). According to this rubric, the assignment is worth 20 marks based on four criteria:

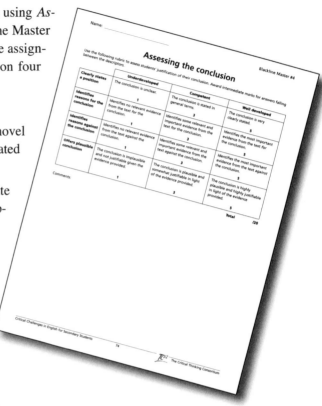

- states a clear position;

- provides evidence from the novel that might challenge the stated position;

- provides ample and accurate evidence from the novel in support of the stated position;

- offers a plausible conclusion given the evidence provided.

Extension

➤ Distinguish between a good and an effective leader. Consider whether Jack or Ralph is more effective as a leader.

➤ Evaluate Piggy's leadership qualities using the same process and determine whether Piggy could have emerged as a leader?

Reference

Golding, William. (1954). *Lord of the Flies*. London: Faber & Faber.

Leadership profiles

Names of school leaders	Leadership qualities

Names of community leaders	Leadership qualities

Names of national/ international leaders	Leadership qualities
Martin Luther King, Jr.	*He stood up for his beliefs even when they were unpopular.*

Jack's and Ralph's leadership

List the five most important attributes of good leadership in the column on the left. Look for evidence from the novel that suggests whether or not Jack and Ralph possess these attributes. Rate the extent to which each character exhibits these attributes on the following scale:

1 = Not at all   2 = Somewhat   3 = Definitely

Leadership qualities	JACK — Evidence from the novel	rating	RALPH — Evidence from the novel	rating
Respect for the ideas and opinions of others	Jack speaks out of turn, disregarding the conch	3 2 (1)	Ralph gives everyone the opportunity to hold the conch and speak	(3) 2 1
		3 2 1		3 2 1
		3 2 1		3 2 1
		3 2 1		3 2 1
		3 2 1		3 2 1

Assessing the ratings

Use the following rubric to assess students' rating of each character's leadership attributes. Award intermediate marks for work that falls between the descriptors.

	Underdeveloped	**Competent**	**Well developed**
Includes relevant evidence	Offers very little relevant evidence from the novel for each attribute. **1**	Offers a few relevant pieces of evidence from the novel for each attribute, but important evidence is sometimes ignored. **3**	Offers several relevant pieces of evidence from the novel for each attribute, including the most important pieces of evidence. **5**
Evidence supports the assigned ratings	The evidence provides does not support any of the ratings. **1**	The evidence provided supports the ratings to some extent, but is sometimes ignored. **3**	The evidence provided strongly supports all of the ratings. **5**

TOTAL   **/ 10**

Comments:

Assessing the conclusion

Use the following rubric to assess students' justification of their conclusion. Award intermediate marks for answers falling between the descriptors.

	Underdeveloped	Competent	Well developed
Clearly states a position	The conclusion is unclear. 1	The conclusion is stated in general terms. 3	The conclusion is very clearly stated. 5
Identifies reasons for the conclusion	Identifies no relevant evidence from the text *for* the conclusion. 1	Identifies some relevant and important evidence from the text *for* the conclusion. 3	Identifies the most important evidence from the text *for* the conclusion. 5
Identifies reasons against the conclusion	Identifies no relevant evidence from the text *against* the conclusion. 1	Identifies some relevant and important evidence from the text *against* the conclusion. 3	Identifies the most important evidence from the text *against* the conclusion. 5
Offers plausible conclusion	The conclusion is implausible and not justifiable given the evidence provided. 1	The conclusion is plausible and somewhat justifiable in light of the evidence provided. 3	The conclusion is highly plausible and highly justifiable in light of the evidence provided. 5

Total   /20

Comments:

Who said words can't kill you?

Critical Challenge

Critical question
Which character in *Lord of the Flies* is the more effective manipulator, Jack or Ralph?

Overview
This is the second of two challenges about leadership based on William Golding's novel *Lord of the Flies*. In this challenge, students learn that the characters who possess the strongest leadership qualities do not necessarily become the most powerful leaders, and that this is also true in real life. Often leaders find ways to become powerful to make up for their leadership deficiencies. Students examine how power can be acquired by using propaganda techniques. They examine the behaviour of Ralph and Jack, the primary leaders in the novel, and study how they use propaganda techniques to enhance their natural leadership skills. Students conclude their analysis by selecting the more effective manipulator and writing a response journal entry explaining their choice.

Objectives

Broad understanding
The most powerful leaders do not necessarily possess the best leadership qualities but may enhance their position using mainpulative means.

Requisite tools

Background knowledge
- familiarity with the novel *The Lord of the Flies*
- techniques of propaganda (e.g., selectivity, repetition, humour)

Criteria for judgment
- criteria for effective manipulation (e.g., effective at convincing others, talented at using the techniques, is successful despite the evidence)

Critical thinking vocabulary
- persuasion
- propaganda
- reasoned argument

Thinking strategies
- data chart

Habits of mind

Suggested Activities

Introduce the idea of manipulation

➤ Present students with the following scenario and ask them to brainstorm in groups what they would do or say to get their way:

> Your family has a strict curfew of 10:00 pm. You desperately want to attend a big rave that starts at 10:00 pm and is sure to run for several hours. How can you persuade them to let you attend?

After 5 or 10 minutes, ask each group to share its methods with the class. Record ideas suggested on the board. Point out that their suggestions are about the strategies people use to try to gain power in everyday life. Further discussion prompts could include how students might manipulate teachers to delay an exam or supervisors to get off work early.

Discuss reasoned argument and propaganda

➤ Distinguish reasoned arguments from propaganda and ask students to provide examples of each. Ask students to analyze and categorize the strategies for persuading people in power listed on the board. Arrange the strategies along a spectrum of persuasion that begins with reasoned arguments and ends with propaganda. Ask students to discuss the line where reasoned argument becomes propaganda (e.g., exaggeration, fear, isolating a foe). Invite students to discuss how we would recognize or identify a person who was good at reasoned argument (e.g., is convincing, provides lot of good reasons, sticks to the truth). Discuss the criteria for recognizing an effective propagandist (e.g., is convincing, uses manipulation instead of reason, is effective despite the truth).

persuasion, reasoned argument and propaganda

Compile list of techniques

➤ Ask students to identify techniques (e.g., exaggeration, fear, isolating a foe) used by propagandists and compile a list on an overhead projector or chalk board. Help students refine wording and clarify the concepts they contribute.

propaganda devices

Review list of techniques

➤ When the student-generated list includes most of the techniques defined in *Propaganda techniques* (Blackline Master #1), distribute this master to students and ask them to highlight the propaganda techniques that emerged in the discussion about ways to manipulate parents in order to attend a party. Ask students to look at the remaining propaganda techniques and identify situations in which they might be used. Add other student-generated techniques to this list.

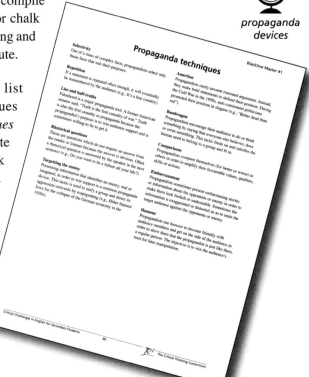

➤ Ask students to work in small groups to identify propaganda techniques used by characters in *Lord of the Flies* and record this information on *Propaganda in* Lord of the Flies (Blackline Master #2).

*familiarity with
the novel*

Session Two

➤ When groups have completed their data charts, explore the following questions in a class discussion:

- Which character stands out as the greater propagandist?

- To what degree are propaganda techniques used successfully?

- What techniques are used most frequently in the novel? Why are they effective?

- How do these techniques enhance the individual leadership styles?

➤ Present the critical question:

Which character in Lord of the Flies *is the more effective manipulator, Jack or Ralph?*

Ask students to justify their choice of the most effective manipulator in a response journal entry or short essay. Remind students to consider the previously-discussed criteria for effective manipulation when supporting their conclusion.

Assess the identification of techniques

➤ Assess students' identification of propaganda techniques using *Assessing the techniques* (Blackline Master #3). According to this rubric, the assignment is worth 10 marks based on two criteria:

- correct identification of propaganda devices;

- use of quotes, examples or references to illustrate technique.

Assess the essay

➤ Assess students' essay on the more effective manipulator using *Assessing the paper* (Blackline Master #4). According to this rubric, this assignment is worth 20 marks based on four criteria:

- clearly expresses the student's position on the more effective manipulator;

- identifies the criteria used as the basis for the conclusion;

- offers ample evidence from the novel to support the conclusion;

- is technically proficient with complete sentences, cohesive paragraphs and proper spelling and punctuation.

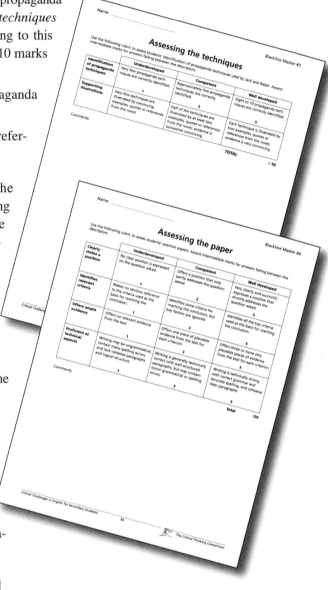

Extension

Design a poster

➤ Ask students to design a campaign poster for one of the leaders in *Lord of the Flies* (Ralph or Jack) that demonstrates that character's ability to use propaganda techniques. Ask students to include both a slogan and a visual display. Evaluate these posters on visual effectiveness and the successful use of propaganda techniques.

Mount an election campaign

➤ Hold an election in the class with Jack and Ralph running as opposing candidates. Ask students to write election speeches, write campaign pamphlets and design television advertisements. Evaluate students on the effective use of propaganda devices to persuade the electorate.

Apply to other novels

➤ Adapt this lesson to other novels that focus on characters who manipulate others using propaganda devices (such as *Animal Farm* and *1984* by George Orwell).

➤ If students have now completed both critical challenges on *Lord of the Flies*, ask students to combine the idea of leadership qualities and effective manipulation into a longer writing assignment based on the critical question: Which character in *Lord of the Flies* is the better overall leader, Jack or Ralph?

Reference

Golding, William. (1954). *Lord of the Flies*. London: Faber & Faber.

Propaganda techniques

Selectivity

Out of a mass of complex facts, propagandists select only those facts that suit their purposes.

Repetition

If a statement is repeated often enough, it will eventually be remembered by the audience (e.g., It's a free country).

Lies and half-truths

Falsehood is a major propaganda tool. A former American senator said, "Truth is the first casualty of war." Truth is also the first casualty in propaganda because the propagandist's purpose is to win audience support and is sometimes willing to lie to get it.

Rhetorical questions

These are questions which do not require an answer from the reader or listener because the answer is obvious. Often a rhetorical question is answered by the speaker in the next sentence (e.g., Do you want to be a failure all your life?).

Targetting the enemy

Presenting information that identifies an enemy, real or imagined, in order to win support is a common propaganda device. This tactic is used to unify a group and direct its aggression outwards by scapegoating (e.g., Hitler blamed Jews for the collapse of the German economy in the 1930s).

Assertion

Propagandists rarely present reasoned arguments. Instead, they make bold statements to defend their position. During the Cold War in the 1950s, anti-communist politicians promoted their position in slogans (e.g., "Better dead than red").

Bandwagon

Propagandists encourage their audience to do or think something by saying that everyone else believes, does or owns something. This tactic feeds on and satisfies the human need to belong to a group and fit in.

Comparisons

Propagandists compare themselves (for better or worse) to others in order to amplify their favourable values, qualities, skills or actions.

Embarrassment

Propagandists sometimes present embarrassing stories or information about the opponents or enemy in order to make them look foolish or undesirable. Sometimes the information is exaggerated or distorted so as to unite the target audience against the opponents or enemy.

Humour

Propagandists use humour to become friendly with audience members and get on the side of the audience in order to show them that the propagandist is just like them, a regular person. The objective is to win the audience's trust for later manipulation.

Propaganda in *Lord of the Flies*

J = used by Jack   **R = used by Ralph**

Propaganda device	First example		Second example	
1. Selectivity		J R		J R
2. Repetition		J R		J R
3. Lies and half-truths		J R		J R
4. Rhetorical questions		J R		J R
5. Targetting the enemy		J R		J R
6. Assertion		J R		J R
7. Bandwagon		J R		J R
8. Comparisons		J R		J R
9. Embarrassment		J R		J R
10. Humour		J R		J R

Assessing the techniques

Use the following rubric to assess students' identification of propaganda techniques used by Jack and Ralph. Award intermediate marks for answers falling between the descriptors.

	Underdeveloped	**Competent**	**Well developed**
Identification of propaganda techniques	Very few propaganda techniques are correctly identified. **1**	Approximately five propaganda techniques are correctly identified. **3**	Eight to 10 propaganda techniques are correctly identified. **5**
Supporting illustrations	Very few techniques are illustrated by convincing examples, quotes or references from the novel.	Half of the techniques are illustrated by at least two examples, quotes or references from the novel; evidence is somewhat convincing.	Each technique is illustrated by two examples, quotes or references from the novel; evidence is very convincing.

TOTAL   **/ 10**

Comments:

Assessing the paper

Use the following rubric to assess students' position papers. Award intermediate marks for answers falling between the descriptors.

	Underdeveloped	**Competent**	**Well developed**
Clearly states a position	No clear position is expressed on the question asked. 1	Offers a position that only partly addresses the question asked. 3	Very clearly and succinctly expresses a position that directly addresses the question asked. 5
Identifies relevant criteria	Makes no obvious reference to the criteria used as the basis for reaching the conclusion. 1	Identifies some criteria for reaching the conclusion, but key factors are ignored. 3	Identifies all the key criteria used as the basis for reaching the conclusion. 5
Offers ample evidence	Offers no relevant evidence from the text. 1	Offers one piece of plausible evidence from the text for each criterion. 3	Offers three or more very plausible pieces of evidence from the text for each criterion. 5
Proficient at technical aspects	Writing may be ungrammatical, contain many spelling errors, and lack cohesive paragraphs and logical structure. 1	Writing is generally technically correct with well structured paragraphs, but may contain minor grammatical or spelling errors. 3	Writing is technically strong with correct grammar and accurate spelling, and cohesive, clear paragraphs. 5

Total   /20

Comments:

A question of pride?

Critical Challenge

Critical question

A. Was Al a fool for turning down the job?

B. Develop effective counter-arguments to support your position.

Overview

In this two-part challenge, students explore the complex array of conflicting arguments that the protagonist Al Condraj must consider when making a moral decision in the short story *The Parsley Garden* by William Saroyan. The plot involves a young man from a low income, single parent family who steals a hammer. He feels ashamed and humiliated by his action and, after working off his debt, he is faced with the choice to continue working and swallow his pride, or to continue his meagre way of living and keep his value system intact. Students make a judgment about Al's decision not to take a job. They then learn to make counter-arguments before they re-evaluate their initial assessment of Al's decision.

Objectives

Broad understanding

Many decisions about how people should act in given situations raise complex ethical considerations that must be carefully weighed.

Requisite tools

Background knowledge
- familiarity with the short story *The Parsley Garden*

Criteria for judgment
- criteria for a well-supported position (e.g., identifies relevant arguments, offers relevant counter-arguments)
- criteria for effective counter-arguments (e.g., are plausible or realistic, relevant to the argument, provide a compelling alternative or rebuttal)

Critical thinking vocabulary
- counter-argument
- counter counter-argument

Thinking strategies
- data chart

Habits of mind
- open-mindedness

Suggested Activities

Session One

Role play scenarios

➤ Before reading *The Parsley Garden* by William Saroyan, divide the class into four groups. Without any leading comments, give each group one of the following statements and ask them to develop and act out a scene that illustrates the statement.

- You go to your mother for advice and she tells you to "shut up."
- You get caught shoplifting.
- Your boss is rude to you.
- You own a store and theft of your goods is a common problem. You catch someone stealing from you.

Explore the complexity of moral decisions

➤ After each role play, invite students to discuss the choices that were made by characters during the presentation (e.g., you are irate with the thief who stole goods from your store, therefore you yell at her). Then ask students to imagine that there is a plausible, perfectly innocent explanation for the incident. What might this explanation be? Why might it be understandable for a mother to tell a child to "shut up"? Why might shoplifting be justifiable? These role play scenes and the follow-up discussion should elicit the idea that choices may be more complex than they appear on the surface and allow students to empathize with the thoughts and emotions that the characters in the short story experience.

Read short story

➤ Ask students to read the *The Parsley Garden*.

familiarity with the story

Pose the initial critical question

➤ As students finish reading, ask them to write a one-paragraph response (rough copy only) to the critical question:

Was Al a fool for turning down the job?

Session Two   *Blackline Masters #1-2*

Assemble reasons for and against

➤ Designate two students to act as blackboard recorders—one recording the NO side arguments; the other recording the YES side arguments. Begin a discussion in which all students share their reasons for their answer to the critical question.

Introduce counter-arguments

➤ After students have generated various arguments for both sides, introduce the concept of a "counter-argument" and point out that there may be reasons which could explain or counter the justification offered. Illustrate this concept by offering possible counter-arguments to a few of the reasons students offered. Encourage students to offer additional counter-arguments and arguments that counter your counter-arguments. Invite students to consider the following criteria when developing counter-arguments:

counter-arguments and counter counter-arguments

effective counter-arguments

- Are they plausible or realistic claims?
- Are they relevant to the arguments they are intended to counter?

- Do they provide compelling alternatives or rebuttals to the initial arguments?

Introduce the second critical task

➤ Present the second critical challenge:

Develop effective counter-arguments to support your position.

Discuss arguments and counter-arguments

➤ Distribute *No! Al is not a fool* (Blackline Master #1) to those students who supported this view in their one paragraph response and distribute *Yes! Al is a fool* (Blackline Master #2) to those holding the opposing view. Divide students into small groups, ensuring where possible that there is at least one representative from each side in each group. Students should share the reasons for their choice with the other members of their group. Groups may then consider counter-arguments and arguments that counter the counter-arguments to elicit the most complete picture of the situation possible.

data chart

Complete data charts

➤ Allow students to complete their data charts. Should they wish to change their response to the critical question at this point, give them an opportunity to choose the other blackline master to complete.

Revisit critical question

➤ Invite students to revisit their initial one-paragraph response to the critical question:

Was Al a fool for turning down the job?

open-mindedness

Ask students are to write a more extensive response to the question, in which they focus on exploring arguments and counter-arguments to their position. While revising, encourage students to explain how or why they changed their initial opinion, if they did so. Students should submit their original paragraph and their revised response for evaluation.

Assess the arguments and counter-arguments

➤ Assess students' identification of possible counter-arguments using the rubric *Assessing arguments and counter-arguments* (Blackline Master #3). According to this rubric, the task if worth 15 marks based on three criteria:

- identifies relevant arguments to support their position;

- offers effective and relevant counter-arguments;

- offers effective rebuttals to the counter-arguments.

Assess the final justification

➤ Assess students' justification of their final position using the rubric *Assessing the justification* (Blackline Master #4). According to this rubric, the task if worth 15 marks and is assessed on three criteria:

- identifies relevant reasons for the position;

- identifies relevant counter-arguments to the position;

- offers a convincing justification for the stated position.

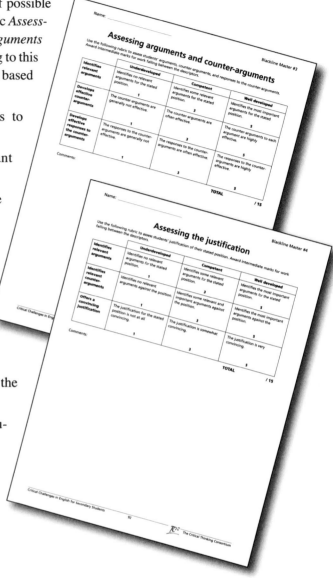

Extension

Write a poem

➤ If students have studied narrative ballads, invite them to write a poem recounting the events in the short story. Students can write this from any character's point of view (e.g., Al Condraj, store owner's, Al's mother).

Develop arguments for a personal decision

➤ Suggest that students identify an important ethical or personal decision they will face in the upcoming months or years and think of reasons for and against possible choices and possible counter-arguments to the reasons they identify.

Reference

Saroyan, William. (1987). "The Parsley Garden". In *Inside Stories I*. (Glen Kirkland & Richard Davies, Eds.) Toronto: Harcourt Brace.

No! Al is not a fool

Possible reasons why Al is NOT a fool	Counter-arguments	Countering the counter-arguments
He's keeping his pride intact by not taking the job.	His family could use the money.	Money isn't the most important thing in life.

Yes! Al is a fool

Possible reasons why Al IS a fool	Counter-arguments	Countering the counter-arguments

Assessing arguments and counter-arguments

Use the following rubric to assess students' arguments, counter-arguments, and responses to the counter-arguments. Award intermediate marks for work falling between the descriptors.

	Underdeveloped	Competent	Well developed
Identifies relevant arguments	Identifies no relevant arguments for the stated position. **1**	Identifies some relevant arguments for the stated position. **3**	Identifies the most important arguments for the stated position. **5**
Develops effective counter-arguments	The counter-arguments are generally not effective. **1**	The counter-arguments are often effective. **3**	The counter-arguments to each argument are highly effective. **5**
Develops effective responses to the counter-arguments	The responses to the counter-arguments are generally not effective. **1**	The responses to the counter-arguments are often effective. **3**	The responses to the counter-arguments are highly effective. **5**

TOTAL   **/ 15**

Comments:

Assessing the justification

Use the following rubric to assess students' justification of their stated position. Award intermediate marks for work falling between the descriptors.

	Underdeveloped	**Competent**	**Well developed**
Identifies relevant arguments	Identifies no relevant arguments *for* the stated position. 1	Identifies some relevant arguments *for* the stated position. 3	Identifies the most important arguments *for* the stated position. 5
Identifies relevant counter-arguments	Identifies no relevant arguments *against* the position. 1	Identifies some relevant and important arguments *against* the position. 3	Identifies the most important arguments *against* the position. 5
Offers a convincing justification	The justification for the stated position is not at all convincing. 1	The justification is somewhat convincing. 3	The justification is very convincing. 5

TOTAL   **/ 15**

Comments:

Who done it?

Critical Challenge

Critical question
Was Moose Maddon's death accidental or deliberate?

Overview
In this challenge, students examine the available evidence and decide whether Moose Maddon's death was accidental or murder. They then write an epilogue to "The Moose and the Sparrow," a story by Hugh Garner, which expresses their opinion. In this story, Cecil is a slight young man who works at a logging camp during his summer breaks from university. Despite his pleasing personality and strong work ethic, Cecil is constantly tormented by Moose Maddon—a man who seems to be threatened by Cecil's intelligence. Moose has an unfortunate mishap and it is uncertain whether Moose's death was accidental or whether Cecil is responsible.

Objectives

Broad understanding
Events can be misunderstood due to ambiguity in the available evidence.

Requisite tools

Background knowledge
- familiarity with the story "The Moose and the Sparrow"

Criteria for judgment
- criteria for plausible theory (e.g., supported with lots of evidence, no unexplained factors, more convincing than alternatives)

Critical thinking vocabulary

Thinking strategies
- data chart

Habits of mind
- attention to detail

    *TC*² The Critical Thinking Consortium

Suggested Activities

Read story

➤ Ask students to read the short story "The Moose and the Sparrow."

familiarity with the story

Discuss Moose's death

➤ Discuss as a class how Moose might have died: accidentally or at Cecil's hands? Invite students to take on the role of detective to solve this problem and remind them that, like all good detectives, they will need to pay close attention to detail. Emphasize the need to consider any shred of evidence and all sources of evidence, including that from all characters.

attention to detail

Compile evidence

➤ Ask each student to compile an ongoing list of evidence that supports both the accident and the murder hypotheses. Distribute copies of *Evidence chart* (Blackline Master #1) so that students may record evidence as they accumulate it.

data chart

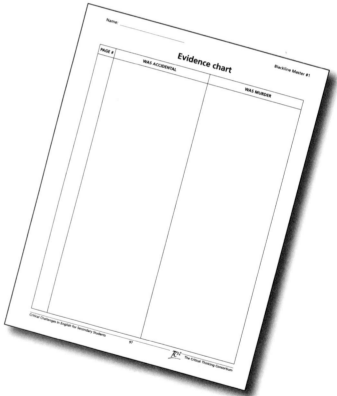

Explore character traits

➤ Suggest that students begin their investigation by exploring the character traits of Cecil and Moose in small groups. Groups may use *Character profile* (Blackline Master #2) to record the traits of both characters, looking for clues about the most plausible explanation for Moose's death.

Consider clues

➤ Invite the groups to consider any clues the narrator of the story (Pop Anderson) provides suggesting that Moose's death might be accidental or, alternatively, that it might be murder.

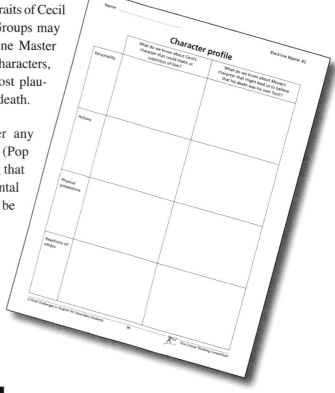

Session Three

Present the critical questions

➤ Once students have collected and recorded the evidence, ask them to consider which hypothesis is the most plausible. Present the critical challenge:

Was Moose Maddon's death accidental or deliberate?

weight of plausible evidence

Discuss evidence

➤ Once students have formed their opinion, arrange the class into a "U-shaped" formation with students who believe the death was accidental on one end, those who believe it was murder on the other, and those who are uncertain in the bottom of the "U." Students may share their ideas about responsibility for Moose's death in an informal debate. (Some guideline for control may be necessary, such as stipulating that only the student holding the chalk brush may speak.) Periodically encourage students to change their position along the "U" if their opinion changes. By the end of the discussion each student should have formed an opinion about the most plausible cause of Moose's death.

Prepare a written justification

➤ After debating the issue, invite students individually to prepare a written justification of their position on the most plausible cause of death. Ask students to focus on three criteria:

criteria for plausible theory

- provide abundant textual evidence to support their preferred theory;

- address all the key elements or questions raised by their theory;

- explain why their position is more plausible than the alternative theory.

Assess the assembled evidence

➤ Assess students' collection of evidence for both theories on the cause of Moose's death using *Assessing the evidence for the theories* (Blackline Master #3). According to this rubric, the assignment is worth 5 marks and is assessed on the amount of relevant textual evidence provided for each of the suspected causes.

Assess the justification

➤ Assess students' justification of the most plausible cause of Moose's death using *Assessing the justification* (Blackline Master #4). According to this rubric, the assignment is worth 15 marks and is assessed on three criteria:

  • provides relevant textual evidence for the suspected cause;

  • addresses all elements of the theory;

  • explains the justification of the identified cause over the alternative theory.

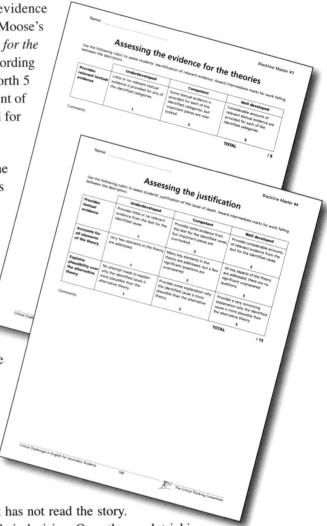

Extension

Conduct a mock trial

➤ Present a mock trial to a jury that has not read the story. Members of the jury must justify their decision. Once the mock trial is over, the jury members should read the story and review their opinion. Do they agree with their verdict, or would they change it?

Write an epilogue

➤ Discuss the meaning and purpose of an epilogue. Students must include evidence from the text to support their view and must write in the same style as the story. Write an epilogue to "The Moose and the Sparrow" explaining the circumstances surrounding Moose Maddon's death.

Reference

Garner, Hugh. (1980). "The Moose and the Sparrow." In *Singing Under Ice* (M. Grace Mersereau, Ed.). Toronto: Gage.

Evidence chart

PAGE #	WAS ACCIDENTAL	WAS MURDER

Character profile

	What do we know about Cecil's character that could make us suspicious of him?	What do we know about Moose's character that might lead us to believe that his death was his own fault?
Personality		
Actions		
Physical possessions		
Reactions of others		

Assessing the evidence for the theories

Use the following rubric to assess students' identification of relevant evidence. Award intermediate marks for work falling between the descriptors.

	Underdeveloped	Competent	Well developed
Provides relevant textual evidence	Little or no relevant textual evidence is provided for any of the identified categories. 1	Some textual evidence is provided for each of the identified categories, but important pieces are overlooked. 3	Considerable amounts of relevant textual evidence are provided for each of the identified categories. 5

TOTAL   / 5

Comments:

Assessing the justification

Use the following rubric to assess students' justification of the cause of death. Award intermediate marks for work falling between the descriptors.

	Underdeveloped	**Competent**	**Well developed**
Provides textual evidence	Provides little or no relevant evidence from the text for the identified cause. 1	Provides some evidence from the text for the identified cause, but important pieces are overlooked. 3	Provides considerable amounts of relevant evidence from the text for the identified cause. 5
Accounts for all elements of the theory	Very few elements in the theory are addressed. 1	Many key elements in the theory are addressed, but a few significant questions are unanswered. 3	All key aspects of the theory are addressed; there are no significant unanswered questions. 5
Explains plausibility over the alternative theory	No attempt made to explain why the identified cause is more plausible than the alternative theory. 1	Provides some explanation why the identified cause is more plausible than the alternative theory. 3	Provides a very convincing explanation why the identified cause is more plausible than the alternative theory. 5

TOTAL   **/ 15**

Comments:

Daytime friends are night time lovers

Critical Challenge

Critical task

Write two versions of Ann's diary entry after her husband's death suggesting differing conclusions, one which points to her infidelity and one to her faithfulness.

Overview

In this challenge, students examine the ambiguity created by Sinclair Ross in his short story, "The Painted Door." This story concerns a couple who are facing marital difficulty. Ann, the wife, is attracted to her husband's friend, Steven. As the story progresses Sinclair Ross is deliberately ambiguous about Ann's fidelity. Students discuss what it means to be unfaithful and then examine Ann's fidelity or lack thereof. By doing this, students also learn more about counter-argument. In the culminating activity students write two diary entries from Ann's point of view: one which points to her infidelity and the other which points to her fidelity.

Objectives

Broad understanding

There are two sides to every story, and ambiguity can make the truth difficult to ascertain.

Requisite tools

Background knowledge
- familiarity with the story "The Painted Door"

Criteria for judgment
- criteria for infidelity (e.g., intentionally hurtful to others, act behind others' backs)

Critical thinking vocabulary
- counter-argument
- inference

Thinking strategies
- data chart
- pro and con chart

Habits of mind
- open-mindedness

Suggested Activities

Read story

➤ Assign reading "The Painted Door" by Sinclair Ross as homework.

familiarity with the story

Develop criteria for fidelity

➤ Ask students to think of an occasion when a friend was unfaithful to them. Frame unfaithfulness broadly to include examples such as a friend telling a secret to a third party, boyfriend/girlfriend break-up, a friend not keeping a commitment, and so on.

features of being unfaithful

In a class discussion or in small groups ask students to brainstorm key aspects of infidelity. Suggest some of the following features:

- an action done with the intention of hurting another person;
- an action done behind someone's back;
- an attack on a belief or event that a person values highly;
- a violation of a mutual understanding between the two individuals.

Create a class list on the board of criteria to test infidelity.

Define and list criteria for unfaithfulness

➤ Ask students to write a personal definition of the word and a list of criteria to test unfaithfulness. Explain that later they will be able to to add qualifications to this definition or modify it.

Explore sample scenarios

➤ Organize a "human graph" to engage students in a further exploration of the fine line between faithfulness and unfaithfulness. On a long wall in the classroom, post the numbers 1 through 5, creating five zones. Present each of the following questions and ask students to stand at the position that corresponds to their belief. Assign Number 1 to be the position of strongest agreement and Number 5 to be the position of strongest disagreement. Once students have lined up in front of the number most closely representing their positions, a human graph will be evident to the class. Follow each question with an opportunity for students to justify their position on the human graph and a chance to reposition themselves after hearing others speak. After each question ask students to discuss how their present position fits their criteria for unfaithfulness.

open-mindedness

Would you consider your spouse or partner to be unfaithful if . . .

- he/she shared intimate thoughts with a person outside the relationship?
- he/she admitted an attraction to a person of the opposite sex?
- he/she admitted fantasizing about someone of the opposite sex?
- he/she had sex with another partner?

Use the results of this discussion to modify or add to the class list of criteria created earlier.

Review criteria

➤ Ask students to review their personal definition and list of criteria for unfaithfulness. Explain that this lesson will use the class-generated criteria for the term "unfaithful" to judge Ann's infidelity. Ask students to copy the class-established criteria.

Introduce inference

➤ Discuss the ambiguity in the Sinclair Ross story and introduce the concept of inference. Ask students to complete *Ann's unfaithfulness* (Blackline Master #1A-B) using the criteria established by the class, and determine whether Ann was unfaithful to John. Ask students to provide quotations from the text that support their opinions.

data chart

Introduce counter-argument

➤ After sharing some of their findings, introduce and define counter-argument. Ask students to find one quote to support the other side and record this on *Ann's unfaithfulness* (Blackline Master #1A-B) as well.

counter-argument

Record opposing evidence

➤ Create a T-chart on the chalkboard or an overhead transparency. Label the first column *Ann is faithful* and a second column *Ann is unfaithful*. Complete the T-chart with the quotations students have found.

data chart

Discuss as a class

➤ Once the quotations are on the chalkboard or an overhead transparency, ask students to take one of the two positions. It may be necessary to allow a position for those students who are undecided. Arrange classroom seating so that people who have chosen each of these positions are seated in one group or the other. This could be done as a U-shaped discussion. Discuss the quotes on the board and ask students to defend their positions. Present counter-arguments by using the criteria in the chart (for example, "Did Ann know her action would hurt her husband?").

Allow students to change positions throughout the discussion. Point out that some quotes may appear to support both sides of the T-chart, and discuss Ross's use of ambiguity.

Present the critical task

➤ After students have had an opportunity to discuss their positions, direct them to return to their usual classroom seats and present the critical task:

Write two versions of Ann's diary entry after her husband's death suggesting differing conclusions, one which points to her infidelity and one to her faithfulness.

Encourage students to support each position with material from the story.

Evaluation   *Blackline Masters #2-3*

Assess the evidence collected

➤ Assess students' completed blackline masters using *Assessing the evidence* (Blackline Master #2). According to this rubric, the task is worth 10 marks based on the following criteria:

- identifies relevant actions and thoughts;

- clearly explains how the action and thoughts suggest faithfulness/un-faithfulness to her husband.

Assess the competing versions

➤ Assess students' diary entries using *Assessing the competing versions* (Blackline Master #3). According to this rubric, the assignment is worth 10 marks based on the following criteria:

- incidents in the text are used to explain each version of the story;

- both versions are convincingly written from Ann's perspective.

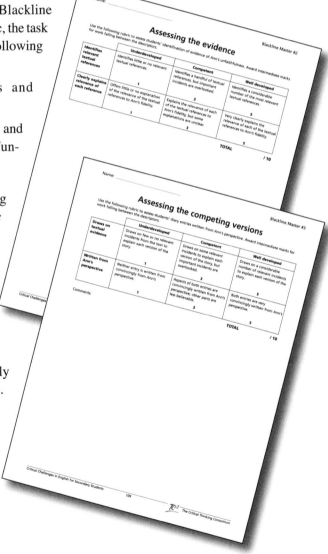

Explore the use of ambiguity

➤ Ask students to reflect on the following questions either in discussion or writing:

- What are some benefits of writing ambiguously?

- Are there occasion when ambiguity is acceptable? Desirable?

- What type of story development requires ambiguity?

Write an ambiguous story

➤ Write a story that has a purposely ambiguous development.

References

The text version of *The Painted Door* by Sinclair Ross can be found in many anthologies. Two easily available sources are:

Kirkland, Glen and Davies, Richard. (1993). *Inside Stories For Senior Students*. Toronto: Harcourt Brace.

MacNeill and Sorestad. (1973). *Tigers of the Snow*. Scarborough, ON: Nelson Canada.

Ann's unfaithfulness

Instructions: For each of the criteria established for unfaithfulness explain whether or not Ann was being unfaithful to John.

ANN'S ACTIONS AND THOUGHTS	CRITERIA FOR UNFAITHFULNESS			
	Are intended to hurt person	Are carried out behind the person's back	Attack the person's beliefs	Violate mutual understanding
Dances with Steven at the barn dance				
Allows Steven to visit in John's absence				
"her eyes were fanatic, believing desperately, fixed upon him as if to exclude all else, as if to find justification				

				ANN'S ACTIONS AND THOUGHTS	
				Are intended to hurt person	
				Are carried out behind the person's back	CRITERIA FOR UNFAITHFULNESS
				Attack the person's beliefs	
				Violate mutual understanding	

Assessing the evidence

Use the following rubric to assess students' identification of evidence of Ann's unfaithfulness. Award intermediate marks for work falling between the descriptors.

	Underdeveloped	**Competent**	**Well developed**
Identifies relevant textual references	Identifies little or no relevant textual references. **1**	Identifies a handful of textual references, but important incidents are overlooked. **3**	Identifies a considerable number of the most relevant textual references. **5**
Clearly explains relevance of each reference	Offers little or no explanation of the relevance of the textual references to Ann's fidelity. **1**	Explains the relevance of each of the textual references to Ann's fidelity, but some explanations are unclear. **3**	Very clearly explains the relevance of each of the textual references to Ann's fidelity. **5**

TOTAL   / 10

Assessing the competing versions

Use the following rubric to assess students' diary entries written from Ann's perspective. Award intermediate marks for work falling between the descriptors.

	Underdeveloped	**Competent**	**Well developed**
Draws on textual evidence	Draws on few or no relevant incidents from the text to explain each version of the story. 1	Draws on some relevant incidents to explain each version of the story, but important incidents are overlooked. 3	Draws on a considerable number of relevant incidents to explain each version of the story. 5
Written from Ann's perspective	Neither entry is written convincingly from Ann's perspective. 1	Aspects of both entries are convincingly written from Ann's perspective; other parts are less believable. 3	Both entries are very convincingly written from Ann's perspective. 5

TOTAL   **/ 10**

Comments:

Baseball is life . . . the rest is just details

Critical Challenge

Critical question

Is the metaphor "baseball is life" suggested by the poem "The Base Stealer" a powerful one?

Overview

In this critical challenge, students explore the idea that a poem can serve as an extended metaphor. "The Base Stealer," a poem by Robert Francis ostensibly describes a crucial type of play in baseball. It can also be read as a metaphor for many other things—life, decision-making and growing up. Students read the poem with the title removed, hypothesize what it is about, and then explore the effectiveness of the poem as an extended metaphor. They do this by looking for the parallels between the poem and life and by assessing the metaphor in light of agreed-upon criteria.

Objectives

Broad understanding

Extended metaphors can offer illuminating insights about the object of comparison.

Requisite tools

Background knowledge
- familiarity with the poem "The Base Stealer"
- understanding metaphor

Criteria for judgment
- criteria for a powerful metaphor (e.g., is apt, offers insight, is original)

Critical thinking vocabulary

Thinking strategies
- comparison chart

Habits of mind

Suggested Activities

Introduce the poem

➤ On an overhead projector, display "The Base Stealer," a poem by Robert Francis, with its title removed. Ask students to read the poem. A copy of this poem is reprinted on *"Untitled poem"* (Blackline Master #1).

knowledge of the poem

Brainstorm title

➤ Divide students into small groups and ask each group to brainstorm a title for this poem that reflects the content, theme or mood of the poem. Distribute chart paper and ask each group to record its suggested title and quotations from the poem to support the choice.

> Read the following poem. Decide on a suitable title for this poem.
>
> **Untitled** *Blackline Master #1*
>
> Poised between going on and back, pulled
> Both ways taut like a tightrope-walker,
> Fingertips pointing the opposites,
> Now bouncing tiptoe like a dropped ball
> Or a kid skipping rope, come on, come on,
> Running a scattering of steps sidewise,
> How he teeters, skitters, tingles, teases,
> Taunts them, crowd him, hovers like an ecstatic bird,
> He's only flirting, crowd him, crowd him,
> Delicate, delicate, delicate, delicate—now!
>
> —*Robert Francis*

Reveal title

➤ Post each group's chart paper on the classroom wall, and discuss the suggested titles and the supporting quotations provided. Announce the original title and invite students to discuss how it fits the poem.

Critical Challenges in English for Secondary Students 116 *The Critical Thinking Consortium*

Review metaphor

➤ Review what a metaphor is. Discuss whether or not "The Base Stealer" is explicitly about a baseball player. Ask students to look beyond the literal meaning and suggest metaphorical interpretations of the poem.

knowledge of metaphor

Analyze the poem

➤ Ask students to complete the first three columns of *Metaphorical Analysis of "The Base Stealer"* (Blackline Master #2) to demonstrate an understanding of how the poem works on two levels of meaning. Students should look for quotes from the poem and indicate parallels between baseball and life.

comparison chart

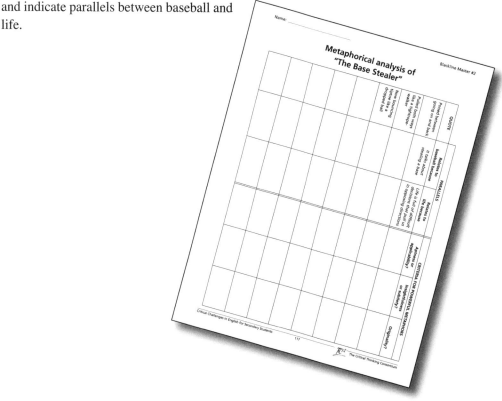

Session Two

Criteria for metaphor

➤ Explore with students criteria for determining whether a metaphor is powerful. Possible suggestions include:

- it is apt (Does it apply to the new context?);
- it offers insight (Does it reveal thoughtful or subtle ideas about the topic?);
- it is original (Is it a novel or fresh comparison?).

criteria for powerful metaphor

Evaluate metaphors

➤ Test "The Base Stealer" against the criteria for powerful metaphors. Ask students to complete the remaining columns—Criteria for powerful metaphors—of *Metaphorical analysis of "The Base Stealer"* (Blackline Master #2). Discuss student interpretations as a class.

Pose critical question

➤ Present the critical question:

Is the metaphor "baseball is life" suggested in the poem "The Base Stealer" a powerful one?

Invite students to respond by indicating the degree—along a continuum from "extremely powerful" to "very weak"—to which "baseball is life" is a powerful metaphor. Encourage students to justify their rating in light of the criteria for an effective extended metaphor.

TC² The Critical Thinking Consortium

Assess the data chart

➤ Assess students' completion of *Metaphorical analysis of "The Base Stealer"* (Blackline Master #2) using *Assessing the metaphorical analysis* (Blackline Master #3). According to this rubric, the assignment is worth 15 marks and is assessed on three criteria:

- identify appropriate quotes;

- interpret both the literal and the figurative meaning of the poem;

- provide plausible reasons to support their assessment of how well the parallels between baseball and life meet the criteria of a powerful metaphor.

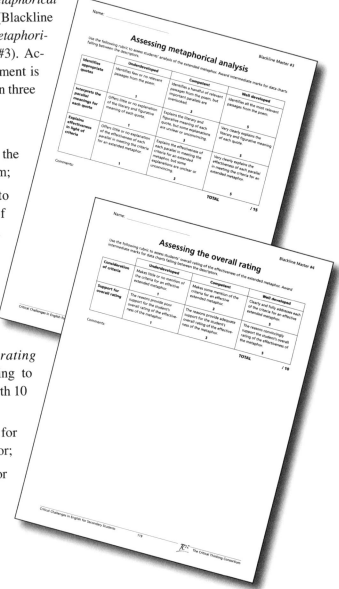

Assess the overall rating

➤ Assess students' justification of the rating of the metaphor using *Assessing the overall rating* (Blackline Master #4). According to this rubric, the assignment is worth 10 marks based on two criteria:

- considers each of the criteria for an effective extended metaphor;

- provides convincing support for the assigned rating.

Extension

Create their own extended metaphor

➤ Ask students to develop an extended metaphor for life in which they demonstrate the ability to write a passage with two different levels of meaning. Remind students to keep the criteria for powerful metaphors in mind. Evaluate their metaphors using the criteria. Suggest that the extended metaphor have an interesting title, offering examples such as:

> Life is a candle . . .
> Life is a salad bar . . .
> Life is a rodeo . . .
> Life is a roller coaster . . .
> Life is a pair of shoes . . .

Arrange for peer evaluation of student-created metaphors, using the criteria for powerful metaphors.

Compare life with another sport

Compare a similar poem

➤ Invite students to write a metaphor for life using "The Base Stealer" as a model, but choosing a sport other than baseball.

➤ Study the poem "Ball Game" by Richard Eberhart and compare it to "The Base Stealer." This poem is found on *Ball Game* (Blackline Master #5).

The Ball Game

Blackline Master #5

Caught off first, he leaped to run to second, but
Then struggled back to first.
He left first because of a natural desire
To leap, to get on with the game.
When you jerk to run to second
You do not necessarily think of a home run.
You want to go on. You want to get to the next stage,
The entire soul is bent on second base.
The fact is that the mind flashes
Faster in action than the muscles can move.
Dramatic! Off first, taut, heading for second,
In a split second, total realization,
Heading for first. Head first! Legs follow fast.
You struggle back to first with victor effort
As, even, after a life of effort and chill,
One flashes back to the safety of childhood,
To that strange place where one had first begun.

—*Richard Eberhart*

Critical Challenges in English for Secondary Students 120 TC² The Critical Thinking Consortium

References

Francis, Robert. (1991). "The Base Stealer." In *Departures: Reflections in Poetry* (edited by James Barry). Scarborough, ON: Nelson.

Eberhart, Richard. (1992). "Ball Game." In *Sports in Literature* (edited by Brice Emra). Chicago: National Textbook Company.

Untitled

Read the following poem. Decide on a suitable title for this poem.

Poised between going on and back, pulled
Both ways taut like a tightrope-walker,
Fingertips pointing the opposites.
Now bouncing tiptoe like a dropped ball
Or a kid skipping rope, come on, come on,
Running a scattering of steps sidewise,
How he teeters, skitters, tingles, teases,
Taunts them, hovers like an ecstatic bird,
He's only flirting, crowd him, crowd him,
Delicate, delicate, delicate, delicate—now!

—*Robert Francis*

Metaphorical analysis of "The Base Stealer"

QUOTE	PARALLELS		CRITERIA FOR POWERFUL METAPHORS		
	Relates to baseball because	Relates to life because	Aptness or applicability?	Insightfulness or subtlety?	Originality?
Poised between going on and back	It talks about stealing a base	Life is full of difficult decisions that pull us in opposing directions			
Pulled both ways like a tightrope-walker					
Now bouncing tiptoe like a dropped ball					

Assessing metaphorical analysis

Use the following rubric to assess students' analysis of the extended metaphor. Award intermediate marks for data charts falling between the descriptors.

	Underdeveloped	**Competent**	**Well developed**
Identifies appropriate quotes	Identifies few or no relevant passages from the poem. **1**	Identifies a handful of relevant passages from the poem, but important parallels are overlooked. **3**	Identifies all the most relevant passages from the poem. **5**
Interprets the parallel meanings for each quote	Offers little or no explanation of the literary and figurative meaning of each quote. **1**	Explains the literary and figurative meaning of each quote, but some explanations are unclear or unconvincing. **3**	Very clearly explains the literary and figurative meaning of each quote. **5**
Explains effectiveness in light of criteria	Offers little or no explanation of the effectiveness of each parallel in meeting the criteria for an extended metaphor. **1**	Explains the effectiveness of each parallel in meeting the criteria for an extended metaphor, but some explanations are unclear or unconvincing. **3**	Very clearly explains the effectiveness of each parallel in meeting the criteria for an extended metaphor. **5**

TOTAL   **/ 15**

Comments:

Assessing the overall rating

Use the following rubric to assess students' overall rating of the effectiveness of the extended metaphor. Award intermediate marks for data charts falling between the descriptors.

	Underdeveloped	Competent	Well developed
Consideration of criteria	Makes little or no mention of the criteria for an effective extended metaphor. 1	Makes some mention of the criteria for an effective extended metaphor. 3	Clearly and fully addresses each of the criteria for an effective extended metaphor. 5
Support for overall rating	The reasons provide poor support for the student's overall rating of the effectiveness of the metaphor. 1	The reasons provide adequate support for the student's overall rating of the effectiveness of the metaphor. 3	The reasons convincingly support the student's overall rating of the effectiveness of the metaphor. 5

TOTAL   **/ 10**

Comments:

The Ball Game

Caught off first, he leaped to run to second, but

Then struggled back to first.

He left first because of a natural desire

To leap, to get on with the game.

When you jerk to run to second

You do not necessarily think of a home run.

You want to go on. You want to get to the next stage,

The entire soul is bent on second base.

The fact is that the mind flashes

Faster in action than the muscles can move.

Dramatic! Off first, taut, heading for second,

In a split second, total realization,

Heading for first. Head first! Legs follow fast.

You struggle back to first with victor effort

As, even, after a life of effort and chill,

One flashes back to the safety of childhood,

To that strange place where one had first begun.

—Richard Eberhart

Pushing the poetic envelope

Critical Challenge

Critical task

Design a concrete poem that arranges words visually to communicate the theme of the poem.

Overview

In this challenge, students explore concrete poetry—a form of poetry that arranges words to create a visual picture that enhances the poem's impact. Students consider a definition of poetry and the boundaries of poetic form, and learn how at times in the past, poetic form has been more rigidly defined. They explore how the visual arrangement of a poem can contribute to and enhance or even create its meaning. Ultimately, students author their own concrete poem.

Objectives

Broad understanding

The boundaries of poetic form continually expand. Words can create a visual picture that enhances the meaning of a poem.

Requisite tools

Background knowledge
- knowledge of concrete poetry
- knowledge of traditional poetic forms, including free verse

Criteria for judgment
- criteria for a concrete poem (e.g., arranged words enhance the meaning, is playful)

Critical thinking vocabulary

Thinking strategies

Habits of mind

Suggested Activities

Explore elements of poetry

➤ Divide students into small groups and ask the groups to recall an example of poetry. Give the groups 2–3 minutes to brainstorm examples, then ask them to read or show their examples to the class. Students may quote a familiar poem or rhyme, or they may create an original poem. As each group presents its poem, discuss the poetic elements present in their example (such as rhyme, meter, stanza structure, imagery, tone, rhythm, lack of grammatical structure, and so on) and ask students to reflect on how these make a "poem" rather than some other expressive form.

Contrast poetry with other forms

➤ Invite students to contribute to a list of "non-poetry." This list may include:

- novels
- stories
- newspapers
- shopping lists

Ask students to define what poetry is and record the definition your class creates.

Discuss changing poetic form

➤ Ask students whether they are familiar with the great American poet Walt Whitman or know what free verse is. Explain that Whitman is known as the "father" of free verse, a poem with no rhyme scheme. When Whitman first tried publishing his poems, no would accept them for publication. At that time, people believed that poetry by definition rhymed. Whitman paid for the publication of his poems, and ultimately, he altered the way in which poetry is defined. However, America was very slow to appreciate his poetry. Point out to students that this is just one example of poetic form changing through time.

knowledge of traditional forms

Introduce concrete poetry

➤ Explain that poets continue to push at the envelope of poetic form. Discuss the meaning of the term "concrete" with students and contrast it with the word "abstract." Explain that "concrete poetry" refers to poems where the language of the poem is arranged to create an image or picture showing the central idea of the poem.

Discuss example

➤ Show the first poem "Acrobat" reproduced on *Concrete poems* (Blackline Master #1) on an overhead transparency. Ask students to study this poem and determine the subject or idea expressed in the arrangement of the words.

knowledge of concrete poems

Formulate criteria for concrete poetry

➤ Ask students what the poem expresses about acrobats. Explain that in a concrete poem the image communicates a message that the reader can decode. The message can be conveyed both visually and through the words or sometimes visually only.

Introduce a poem

➤ Hand out copies of *Concrete poems* (Blackline Master #1) to half the class. Ask the students with the blackline masters to read the poem "Like attracts like" to a partner who has not seen the poem.

Discuss the visual element

➤ In a class discussion, ask the students who have not seen the poem to explain what the poem seems to mean. Then ask the students who read the poem to add their interpretation of the poem. Show an overhead of the poem to the whole class and discuss the ways in which poetic value may lie in the visual, rather than being communicated verbally. Note that the form illustrates the meaning of "abstract."

Practice making concrete poems

➤ Ask students to think of an expression, proverb, action word or profession that could be made into a concrete poem. Develop a list of possible items with the class. Divide students into small groups and give them 10 minutes to design a concrete poem based on an item in the list. Provide each group with an overhead transparency on which to record their concrete poem.

Possible ideas may include:
   rock around the clock
   never say never
   all roads lead to Rome
   flirting
   it's raining
   race car driver
   zoo keeper

Share poems

➤ After 10 minutes, ask each group to show their concrete poem to the class on an overhead projector. Discuss concrete and abstract elements from each poem.

Introduce picture poem

➤ Read students any picture poem reproduced on *Picture poetry* (Blackline Master #2) without showing it to them. Ask their opinion of this poem and encourage them to critique it. After some discussion, show them the written form of the poem on an overhead and discuss whether the poem seems richer and more interesting in light of its presentation. Just like a piece of art, the complete idea of a picture poem is only evident when it is seen.

Recreat a picture poem

➤ Hand out a copy of *Picture poetry* (Blackline Master #2) to half the class. Ask students to form pairs in which one student has the master and the other student doesn't. One student is to read the word of the basketball poem and the other will attempt to write the words of the poem into a suitable shape. When students have finished, display each picture poem on the wall and invite students to do a gallery walk where they observe each poem. Discuss the different interpretations and pictures that class members developed.

Criteria for picture poems

➤ Hand-out copies of *Picture poetry* (Blackline Master #2) to all students and discuss the "Giraffe," "Kite," and "Mirror" poems. Ensure that students understand that a picture poem uses descriptive words in a shape that reflects the subject, but the shape is the more significant element. Picture poems are intended to be seen.

criteria for a concrete poem

Present the critical challenge

➤ Assign the critical task

Design a concrete poem that arranges words visually to communicate the theme of the poem.

Assess the poems

➤ Assess students' concrete poems using *Assessing the concrete poem* (Blackline Master #3). According to this rubric, each poem is worth 20 marks based on the following criteria:

- is imaginative;

- is visually appealing;

- contains an abstract idea;

- conveys its message visually.

Name: _____

Assessing the concrete poem

Blackline Master #3

Use the following rubric to assess students' concrete poems. Award intermediate marks for work falling between the descriptors.

	Underdeveloped	Competent	Well developed
Visually appealing	The poem is not visually appealing. 1	The poem has some visual appeal. 3	The poem is visually dramatic or interesting. 5
Imaginative	The words and visual arrangement are very obvious or unoriginal. 1	The words and visual arrangement contain some fresh or original elements. 3	The words and visual arrangement are highly original or fresh. 5
Contains abstract idea	There is little or no message to the poem. 1	The poem communicates a simple idea or message. 3	The poem communicates a thoughtful idea or message. 5
Conveys message visually	The visual arrangement adds little to the content of the poem. 1	The visual arrangement contributes somewhat to the content of the poem. 3	The visual arrangement greatly enhances the content of the poem. 5

Comments:

TOTAL   / 20

Critical Challenges in English for Secondary Students   128   The Critical Thinking Consortium

Extension

Share the poetry

➤ Create a booklet using the concrete poems designed by the class, or organize an Art Gallery Evening inviting parents to view the concrete poems. Alternatively, create greeting cards using concrete poetry.

Concrete poems

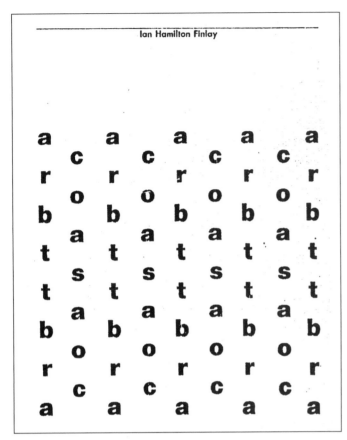

Ian Hamilton Finlay

Emmett Williams

like   attracts   like
like   attracts   like
like   attracts   like
like   attracts   like
like   attracts like
like   attracts like
like attracts like
likeattractslike
likeattractlike
likeattractlike
likattradike
likteralike
liltelikts

Picture poems

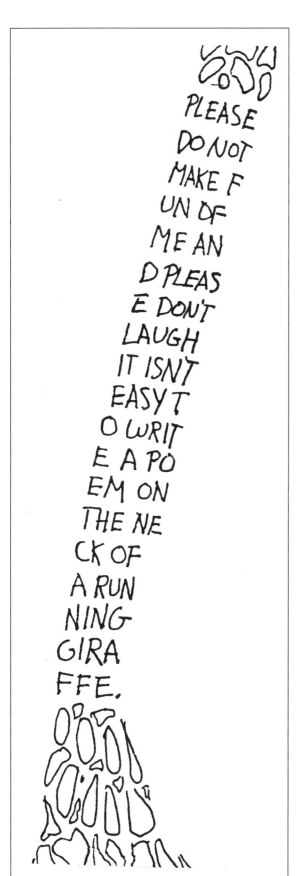

PLEASE
DO NOT
MAKE F
UN OF
ME AN
D PLEAS
E DON'T
LAUGH
IT ISN'T
EASY T
O WRIT
E A PO
EM ON
THE NE
CK OF
A RUN
NING
GIRA
FFE.

Kite

Anonymous

I
wish
I were a
kite on high
I could fly up to the sky
Up to the blue sky
High as a cloud
I wish I were
A kite
High
Up
Up
Up
Up
+
+
+
+
+
+

Assessing the concrete poem

Use the following rubric to assess students' concrete poems. Award intermediate marks for work falling between the descriptors.

	Underdeveloped	**Competent**	**Well developed**
Visually appealing	The poem is not visually appealing. 1	The poem has some visual appeal. 3	The poem is visually dramatic or interesting. 5
Imaginative	The words and visual arrangement are very obvious or unoriginal. 1	The words and visual arrangement contain some fresh or original elements. 3	The words and visual arrangement are highly original or or fresh. 5
Contains abstract idea	There is little or no message to the poem. 1	The poem communicates a simple idea or message. 3	The poem communicates a thoughful idea or message. 5
Conveys message visually	The visual arrangement adds little to the content of the poem. 1	The visual arrangement contributes somewhat to the content of the poem. 3	The visual arrangement greatly enhances the content of the poem. 5

TOTAL   **/ 20**

Comments:

Back to the future

Critical Challenge

Critical task / question

A. Create a comparative collage showing the links between Shakespeare and present times.

B. Which Shakespearean theme is most relevant to modern society?

Overview

In this two-part challenge, students evaluate the degree to which the themes explored in *A Midsummer Night's Dream* (or another Shakespeare play) are applicable to their own lives. Students begin by identifying the themes in a selected Shakespeare play and contemporary society. They create a collage to represent this relationship using newspapers and magazines. Finally they judge which of the themes in the play is most relevant to modern society.

Objectives

Broad understanding

The themes in Shakespearean plays have a universality that makes them as relevant today as they were in the 17th century.

Requisite tools

Background knowledge
- familiarity with *A Midsummer Night's Dream* (or other selected play)
- definition of "theme"

Criteria for judgment
- criteria for a comparative collage e.g., many relevant items, shows links between the compared themes, is engaging or interesing)
- criteria for greatest personal relevance (e.g., widest applicability, most pertinent)

Critical thinking vocabulary

Thinking strategies
- comparison chart

Habits of mind

Suggested Activities

Define "theme"

➤ In a class discussion, review the definition of "theme" and ask students to brainstorm a list of themes found in Shakespeare's *A Midsummer Night's Dream* (or other Shakespearean play). Suggest such themes as parenting, love, power in relationships and the supernatural/magic if they are not raised in discussion.

knowledge of theme and of the play

Compare themes

➤ Ask students to complete the *Theme comparison chart* (Blackline Master #1) beginning with the themes generated in the class discussion. Instruct students to describe in the first column how the theme is treated in the play and in the second column how the same issue is considered in modern society.

comparison chart

Discuss relevant themes

➤ Once completed, discuss the charts with the class. Open the discussion with questions such as:

- Which issues seem the easiest to link between the past and present?

- Which issues seem the most difficult to link between the past and present?

Present the first critical challenge

➤ Introduce the critical task:

Create a comparative collage showing the links between Shakespearean and present times.

Discuss with the class the criteria for an effective comparative collage:

- contains many relevant items or features;

- clearly shows the links between the two periods;

- is revealing or interesting.

criteria for a comparative collage

Create collages

➤ Divide students into small groups. Provide each group with scissors, current newspapers and news magazines, glue, and a large piece of construction paper. Direct each group to search through the newspapers and news magazines to find articles, headlines and/or pictures referring to current issues and to use them to compose a "now and then" collage that illustrates the links between the present and Shakespearean times. (An additional class period may be required for students to complete this task.)

Session Two

Display collages

➤ When the collages are completed, ask groups to display them and explain their choice of clippings.

Determine relevance today

➤ Ask students to complete *Comparing Shakespeare's time with the present* (Blackline Master #2). Use the completed masters as a foundation for a discussion to determine which Shakespearean theme has the greatest relevance today. Invite students to consider which of these themes has the most extensive and pertinent applicability in contemporary life and why.

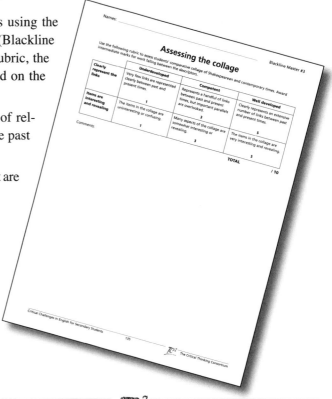

Pose the second critical challenge

➤ Pose the critical question:

Which Shakespearean theme is most relevant to modern society?

Ask students to write a short essay (1–3 pages) in which they explain and defend their choice. Suggest that students explore why their theme is more extensive and pertinent to today's life than any of the other themes.

criteria for personal relevance

Evaluation — Blackline Masters #3-4

Assess the collage

➤ Assess student groups' collages using the rubric *Assessing the collage* (Blackline Master #3). According to this rubric, the collage is worth 10 marks based on the following criteria:

• clearly represents a number of relevant links made between the past and present;

• selects and arranges items that are interesting and revealing.

➤ Assess the short essays using the rubric *Assessing personal relevance* (Blackline Master #4). According to this rubric, the short essay is worth 10 marks based on the following criteria:

- provides convincing reasons for the relevance of the identified themes;
- explains why the identified theme is more relevant than any of the other themes.

Extension

➤ Hold a debate with the resolution: "A Midsummer Night's Dream is still relevant to modern society."

➤ Translate a scene from a Shakespearean play into a modern setting using current English to demonstrate that the play is relevant to contemporary society.

References

William Shakespeare. *A Midsummer Nights' Dream.*

Theme comparison chart

	SHAKESPEARE'S TIME	CONTEMPORARY SOCIETY
Parenting		
Love		
Power		
Supernatural		

Comparing Shakespeare's time
with the present

SIMILARITIES	DIFFERENCES
Parenting in Shakespeare's time is *similar* to today because	*Parenting* in Shakespeare's time is *different* from today because
Love in Shakespeare's time is *similar* to today because	*Love* in Shakespeare's time is *different* from today because
Power in Shakespeare's time is *similar* to today because	*Power* in Shakespeare's time is *different* from today because
The *supernatural* in Shakespeare's time is *similar* to today because	The *supernatural* in Shakespeare's time is *different* from today because

Assessing the collage

Use the following rubric to assess students' comparative collage of Shakespearean and contemporary times. Award intermediate marks for work falling between the descriptors.

	Underdeveloped	Competent	Well developed
Clearly represent the links	Very few links are represented clearly between past and present times. **1**	Represents a handful of links between past and present times, but important parallels are overlooked. **3**	Clearly represents an extensive number of links between past and present times. **5**
Items are interesting and revealing	The items in the collage are uninteresting or confusing. **1**	Many aspects of the collage are somewhat interesting or revealing. **3**	The items in the collage are very interesting and revealing. **5**

TOTAL   / 10

Comments:

Assessing personal relevance

Use the following rubric to assess students' justification of the most relevant theme. Award intermediate marks for work falling between the descriptors.

	Underdeveloped	**Competent**	**Well developed**
Provides convincing reasons	Provides no convincing reasons for the relevance of the identified theme. 1	Provides a few reasons for the relevance of the identified theme, but important issues are overlooked. 3	Provides very convincing reasons for the relevance of the identified theme. 5
Explains relevance over other themes	No attempt is made to explain why the identified theme is more relevant than any of the other themes. 1	Provides some explanation why the identified theme is more relevant than the other themes. 3	Provides very convincing explanations why the identified theme is more relevant than all of the other themes. 5

TOTAL   **/ 10**

Comments:

Fate or free will?

Critical Challenge

Critical question

To what extent are Romeo and Juliet victims of fate?

Overview

In this critical challenge, students assess the extent to which Romeo and Juliet are victims of fate rather than the authors of their own misfortune. Shakespeare's *Romeo and Juliet* is a romantic tragedy that focusses on the lives of two teenagers from feuding families who meet and fall in love. The long-standing feud between their families makes a relationship between these two lovers highly problematic, and a sequence of events unfolds in the play which leads to their tragic deaths. Students consider to what degree these events were caused by fate (circumstances beyond their control) or by free will (the result of their own decisions).

Objectives

Broad understanding

In many circumstances it is not obvious the extent to which individuals are agents of their own free will or victims of factors beyond their control.

Requisite tools

Background knowledge
- familiarity with Shakespeare's *Romeo and Juliet*

Criteria for judgment
- criteria for free will (e.g., circumstances within the individual's control, able to exercise choice)

Critical thinking vocabulary

Thinking strategies
- rating scale

Habits of mind

Suggested Activities

List major events

➤ As a class invite students to identify some of the major events in their lives (e.g., winning a team championship, taking a special trip, undergoing major surgery, achieving a personal goal).

rating scale

Analyze one event

➤ When the list is sufficiently developed, ask students to select one event from the list and complete the first two columns of *Major event lead-up* (Blackline Master #1). Direct them to analyze the major event in terms of a series of lesser events leading to the end result. As illustrated below, ask students to explain why or how each minor event is linked to the major event.

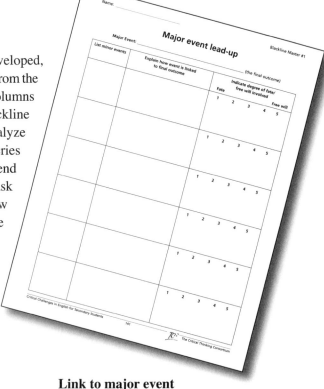

Minor event	Link to major event
Mr. Harvey was my grade 8 basketball coach	*His excellent coaching helped me learn proper skills at a young age and thus I was able to develop more fully which made it possible to play at a competitive level.*

Define fate and free will

➤ Introduce and discuss the concepts of fate (circumstances beyond an individual's control) and free will (actions resulting directly from an individual's choices). Invite students to suggest some simple, everyday examples of fate (e.g., The electricity fails overnight, your electric alarm does not go off at the right time and you miss a test) and of free will (e.g., Because you chose to go to a movie instead of studying for a test, you are ill-prepared and therefore fail the test.). Invite students to volunteer events they have listed on their data charts and indicate to what extent these minor events are instances of free will or of fate.

Encourage students to see that free will and fate exist at opposite ends of a continuum and that it is likely that elements of fate and free will co-exist in many events.

criteria for free will

➤ Revisit Blackline Master #1 and ask students to complete the third column by indicating the degree to which each minor event is the result of free will or of fate. Conclude the activity by inviting students to present and discuss the elements of fate or free will in various minor events listed on their data charts.

Session Two   *Blackline Master #2*

Analyze play

➤ Divide students into pairs or groups of three to analyze the role of fate and free will in *Romeo and Juliet* by completing *Fate or free will?* (Blackline Master #2A-B). Instruct students to complete column one by describing an event from the specified scenes that eventually led to the death of Romeo or Juliet.

rating scale

knowledge of the play

Ask students to describe events from scenes of their choice on the second page of *Fate or free will?* Next, students are to indicate how or why the events contributed to the deaths of Romeo or Juliet in column two. In column three, students are to indicate the degree to which the event is the result of fate or free will.

Pose the critical question

➤ After students have completed Blackline Master #2, present the critical question:

To what extent are Romeo and Juliet victims of fate?

In the pairs or small groups previously arranged, students must decide their overall rating on how strongly fate influences the outcome of the play.

Discuss results

➤ Ask a representative from each group to share its conclusion with the class. Discuss any disagreements about whether events are the result of fate or free will, and invite students to justify their overall rating of the play's outcome.

Assess the contributing events

➤ Assess students' identification of the events leading to the final outcome using *Assessing the contributing events* (Blackline Master #3). According to this rubric, the assignment is worth 15 marks, based on the following criteria:

- identifies relevant events;

- explains links between events and final outcome;

- offers plausible justifications for fate/free will ratings provided.

Assess the overall conclusion

➤ Assess students' overal rating of the degree of free will/fate using the rubric *Assessing the degree of free will* (Blackline Master #4). According to this rubric, the assignment is worth 10 marks, and is assessed on two criteria:

- includes relevant textual evidence;

- offers reasons that convincingly support the overall assessment.

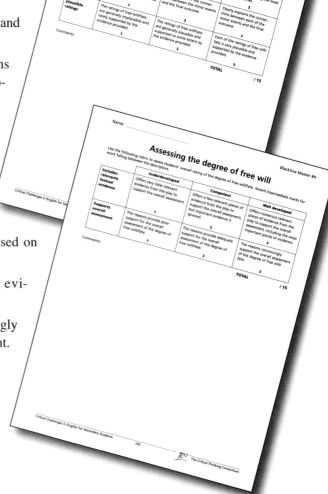

Extension

Alter the outcome

➤ Ask students to alter a few minor events in Romeo and Juliet and then write a summary version of the play illustrating how the alteration of an event could change the outcome of the story.

Explore the tragedy of the play

➤ Discuss the term "tragedy" as understood by students. Present the class with the definition found in a literary reference book (e.g., K. Beckson and A. Ganz, *Literary Terms: A Dictionary*, 1975). Discuss whether or not Romeo and Juliet should be classified as a tragedy.

Major event lead-up

Major Event: _____ (the final outcome)

List minor events	Explain how event is linked to final outcome	Indicate degree of fate/ free will involved
		Fate Free will 1 2 3 4 5
		1 2 3 4 5
		1 2 3 4 5
		1 2 3 4 5
		1 2 3 4 5
		1 2 3 4 5

Fate or free will?

Describe minor events	Explain how it contributed to the deaths of Romeo or Juliet	Indicate degree of fate/ free will involved				
		Fate				Free will
Act. 1, Scene 5		1	2	3	4	5
Act. 2, Scene 2		1	2	3	4	5
Act. 2, Scene 3		1	2	3	4	5
Act. 2, Scene 6		1	2	3	4	5
Act. 3, Scene 1		1	2	3	4	5

Describe minor events	Explain how it contributed to the deaths of Romeo or Juliet	Indicate degree of fate/ free will involved				
		Fate				Free will
Act. ___, Scene ___		1	2	3	4	5
Act. ___, Scene ___		1	2	3	4	5
Act. ___, Scene ___		1	2	3	4	5
Act. ___, Scene ___		1	2	3	4	5
Act. ___, Scene ___		1	2	3	4	5

Assessing the contributing events

Use the following rubric to assess students' identification, explanation and rating of the contributing events. Award intermediate marks for work falling between the descriptors.

	Underdeveloped	**Competent**	**Well developed**
Identifies relevant minor events	Few relevant minor events are mentioned. **1**	A number of minor events are mentioned, but significant ones are missing. **3**	Many relevant minor events are mentioned, including the most significant ones. **5**
Clearly explains the link to the final outcome	Offers little or no explanation of the connections between the minor events and the final outcome. **1**	Explains many of the connections between the minor events and the final outcome. **3**	Clearly explains the connections between each of the minor events and the final outcome. **5**
Offers plausible ratings	The ratings of free will/fate are generally implausible and rarely supported by the evidence provided. **1**	The ratings of free will/fate are generally plausible and supported to some extent by the evidence provided. **3**	Each of the ratings of free will/fate is very plausible and supported by the evidence provided. **5**

TOTAL   / 15

Comments:

Assessing the degree of free will

Use the following rubric to assess students' overall rating of the degree of free will/fate. Award intermediate marks for work falling between the descriptors.

	Underdeveloped	**Competent**	**Well developed**
Includes relevants textual evidence	Offers very little relevant evidence from the play to support the overall assessment. **1**	Offers a few relevant pieces of evidence from the play to support the overall assessment, but important evidence is ignored. **3**	Offers numerous relevant pieces of evidence from the play to support the overall assessment, including the most important pieces of evidence. **5**
Supports overall assessment	The reasons provide poor support for the overall assessment of the degree of free will/fate. **1**	The reasons provide adequate support for the overall assessment of the degree of free will/fate. **3**	The reasons convincingly support the overall assessment of the degree of free will/fate. **5**

TOTAL   **/ 15**

Comments:

"Quote, unquote"

Critical Challenge

Critical tasks

A. Rate the significance of the selected quotation.

B. Select two significant quotations that will be presented for identification and analysis in an end-of-unit literature test.

Overview

In this two-part critical challenge, students select quotations to include in an end-of-unit literature test that will ask them to identify the passage and analyze its significance. This challenge can be adapted for use at any grade level with any piece of literature. This particular lesson focusses on Shakespeare's play *Macbeth*. Students explore the criteria for determining significant literary passages and then search an assigned part of the text looking for two quotations that satisfy these criteria. The class then judges the best among those quotes for inclusion in a culminating test for the unit.

Objectives

Broad understanding

Certain passages in a literary work powerfully capture key features of the plot, character and theme.

Requisite tools

Background knowledge
- familiarity with Shakespeare's *Macbeth* (or other play)

Criteria for judgment
- criteria for a significant quotation (e.g., advances the plot, reveals insight about a character, contains strong imagery, addresses a universal theme)

Critical thinking vocabulary

Thinking strategies
- rating chart

Habits of mind

Suggested Activities

Brainstorm criteria

➤ Brainstorm with the class criteria that should be considered when a teacher selects a quotation for a test where students are expected to identify the speaker and the significance of the quoted passage. Ask students what a passage should contain to make it an appropriate quotation for analysis by students. Encourage the class to consider the following criteria:

criteria for quotations

- advances the plot or marks a turning point;

- reveals the qualities of a main character;

- contains strong imagery which adds to the atmosphere of the play;

- describes a theme of universal interest beyond the literary work itself.

Evaluate selected quotations

➤ Divide students into five groups. Prepare and display a transparent overhead of *Quotations from Macbeth* (Blackline Master #1) and distribute a copy of *Evaluating a quotation* (Blackline Master #2) to each student. Assign each group one of the quotations on the overhead transparency and ask them to spend approximately 10 minutes evaluating the assigned quote in light of the criteria just discussed.

knowledge of play

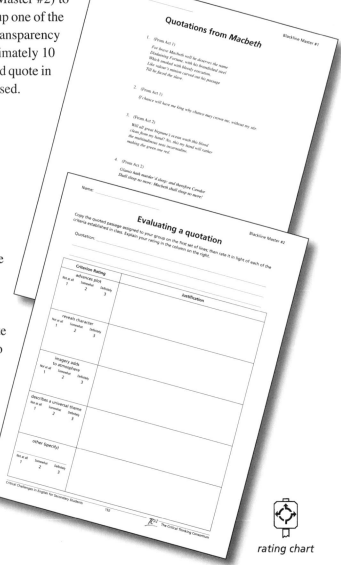

Record and present results

➤ Ask students to record the results of their group's evaluation on their own copy of *Evaluating a quotation* (Blackline Master #2). Invite a member from each group to present the quotation to the whole class and justify the group's rating. Encourage students to comment on the ratings assigned by other groups.

rating chart

Find two passages

➤ Assign each group one act from the play (or from a different play). Ask each group to find one or two new significant passages to recommend for inclusion on an end-of-unit test. Each group is to submit its recommended quote(s) with a page reference and a brief justification in light of the identified criteria. You may suggest that students record their justifications on Blackline Master #2. Prepare a master list of recommended quotations.

Present the second critical challenge

➤ Duplicate and distribute the recommended quotations to each student and present the critical task:

Select two significant quotations that will be presented for identification and analysis in an end-of-unit literature test.

Decide on the best quotations

➤ Ask students to decide upon and justify their votes for the most significant quotations to use on an exam, recording their vote and reasoning on *Student ballot* (Blackline Master #3). Invite students to cast their votes in light of the criteria discussed at the beginning of the lesson. Explain that quotations suggested by students may actually be used on the unit test.

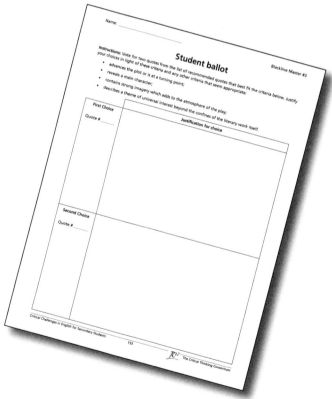

Assess the quotations

➤ Assess students' evaluation of their assigned quotation using the rubric *Assessing the quotations* (Blackline Master #4). According to this rubric, the assignment is worth 10 marks and is assessed on two criteria:

- includes relevant textual evidence;

- offers reasons that convincingly support the ratings for each criterion.

Assess students' selections

➤ Assess student completion of *Student ballot* (Blackline Master #3) using *Assessing the selection* (Blackline Master #5). According to this rubric, the assignment is worth 10 marks based on the following criteria:

- the established criteria are used to justify their selections;

- the reasons provide convincing support for the choices.

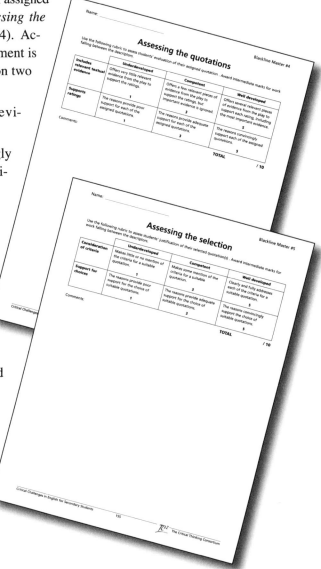

Quotations from *Macbeth*

1. (From Act 1)

    For brave Macbeth well he deserves the name
    Disdaining Fortune, with his brandished steel
    Which smoked with bloody execution,
    Like valour's minion carved out his passage
    Till he faced the slave.

2. (From Act 1)

    If chance will have me king why chance may crown me, without my stir.

3. (From Act 2)

    Will all great Neptune's ocean wash this blood
    clean from my hand? No, this my hand will rather
    the multitudinous seas incarnadine,
    making the green one red.

4. (From Act 2)

    Glamis hath murder'd sleep: and therefore Cawdor
    Shall sleep no more: Macbeth shall sleep no more!

5. (From Act 3)

    Ere we will eat our meal in fear, and sleep
    in the affliction of these terrible dreams
    that shake us nightly: better be with the dead.

Evaluating a quotation

Copy the quoted passage assigned to your group on the first set of lines; then rate it in light of each of the criteria established in class. Explain your rating in the column on the right.

Quotation: _____

_____

_____

Criterion Rating	Justification
advances plot Not at all Somewhat Definitely 1 2 3	
reveals character Not at all Somewhat Definitely 1 2 3	
imagery adds to atmosphere Not at all Somewhat Definitely 1 2 3	
describes a universal theme Not at all Somewhat Definitely 1 2 3	
other (specify) _____ Not at all Somewhat Definitely 1 2 3	

Student ballot

Instructions: Vote for two quotes from the list of recommended quotes that best fit the criteria below. Justify your choices in light of these criteria and any other criteria that seem appropriate:

- advances the plot or is at a turning point;
- reveals a main character;
- contains strong imagery which adds to the atmosphere of the play;
- describes a theme of universal interest beyond the confines of the literary work itself.

	Justification for choice
First Choice Quote # _____	
Second Choice Quote # _____	

Assessing the quotations

Use the following rubric to assess students' evaluation of their assigned quotation. Award intermediate marks for work falling between the descriptors.

	Underdeveloped	Competent	Well developed
Includes relevant textual evidence	Offers very little relevant evidence from the play to support the ratings. **1**	Offers a few relevant pieces of evidence from the play to support the ratings, but important evidence is ignored. **3**	Offers several relevant pieces of evidence from the play to support each rating, including the most important evidence. **5**
Supports ratings	The reasons provide poor support for each of the assigned quotations. **1**	The reasons provide adequate support for each of the assigned quotations. **3**	The reasons convincingly support each of the assigned quotations. **5**

TOTAL   **/ 10**

Comments:

Assessing the selection

Use the following rubric to assess students' justification of their selected quotation(s). Award intermediate marks for work falling between the descriptors.

	Underdeveloped	Competent	Well developed
Consideration of criteria	Makes little or no mention of the criteria for a suitable quotation. **1**	Makes some mention of the criteria for a suitable quotation. **3**	Clearly and fully addresses each of the criteria for a suitable quotation. **5**
Support for choices	The reasons provide poor support for the choice of suitable quotations. **1**	The reasons provide adequate support for the choice of suitable quotations. **3**	The reasons convincingly support the choice of suitable quotations. **5**

TOTAL   **/ 10**

Comments:

The nobler character: Laertes or Hamlet?

Critical Challenge

Critical question

Does Laertes or Hamlet show greater nobility of character?

Overview

In this challenge, students judge which of Laertes or Hamlet shows greater nobility of character. Shakespeare frequently employed characters to serve as foils in his plays. A foil is a character who, by contrast with the protagonist, underscores or enhances the distinctive characteristics of the protagonist. In *Hamlet,* Ophelia's brother Laertes is a foil for Hamlet. Students examine which of Laertes' circumstances are similar to those of Hamlet, and how the two characters react differently to similar circumstances. They consider the features of noble behaviour and then decide whether Hamlet or Laertes has a nobler character.

Objectives

Broad understanding

Authors use certain characters as foils to emphasize aspects of the protagonist's character.

Requisite tools

Background knowledge
- familiar with scenes from *Hamlet* in which Laertes and Hamlet appear
- understand literary use of a character as a foil

Criteria for judgment
- features of a noble character (e.g., acts with honour, rises above petty matters)

Critical thinking vocabulary
- inference

Thinking strategies
- data chart

Habits of mind
- open-mindedness

Suggested Activities

Introduce drama characters

➤ Introduce the concept of dramatic character construction using techniques such as monologue, action and discussion of one character by other characters. Explain how personality traits can be inferred from a character's words or actions. Offer as an example an airplane crash survivor in the wilderness who complains about the difficulties of keeping his hair from looking windblown; such a character could be inferred to be superficial, insecure or vain.

inference

Introduce use of foil

➤ Introduce or review the concept of a character who acts as a foil to another character: a character whose circumstances are in some ways similar to those of the protagonist, but who reacts to them differently. A foil is a way for the author to highlight, through contrast, certain character traits of the protagonist. Explain that Laertes acts as a foil to Hamlet in *Hamlet*. Provide examples of foils from other Shakespearean plays (e.g., Hotspur in *Henry IV*; Mercutio in *Romeo and Juliet*). Ask students to identify similarities between Laertes' and Hamlet's circumstances and describe the ways they react to these circumstances.

character foil

Discuss nobility

➤ In a class discussion, identify and list traits students would expect a noble character to have. Acknowledge and clarify that "noble" has more than one meaning and can refer simply to aristocratic birth as well as to the traits that reveal nobility of character (e.g., acts with honour, rises above petty mattters). If time permits, ask students to develop plausible explanations for the genesis of these alternative definitions. During this discussion, it might be interesting to introduce the concept of *noblesse oblige*.

features of a noble character

Infer character traits

➤ Divide students into groups of three or four to complete *Inferring character traits* (Blackline Master #1). Groups should record significant words or actions of Hamlet or Laertes and list the character traits that can be inferred from these words and actions.

Because *Hamlet* is a lengthy play, and Hamlet appears or is mentioned in almost every scene, it may be practical to have one group analyze Laertes' character (especially I, ii; I, iii; IV, vii; V, ii), and several groups analyze Hamlet's character as revealed at certain points in the play. (One group might be assigned Act I, another Act II and so on.)

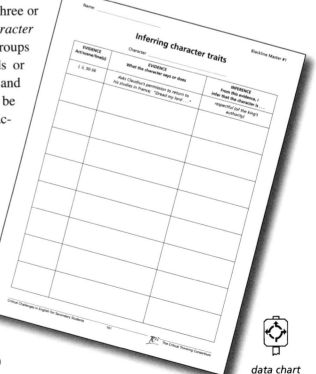

data chart

Session Two

Compare findings within group

➤ Ask groups to compare their completed data charts, noting differences in interpretation and discussing the reasoning that underlies their inferences about the characters' personalities.

Present findings to class

➤ After the group discussion, ask representatives from each group to present their groups' findings and interpretations to the class. Follow this with an open class discussion. Summarize these findings using an overhead projector and ask students to add information from other groups to their own data charts.

Pose the critical question

➤ Direct students to use the accumulated information about the character traits of Laertes and Hamlet as the raw material for a two- or three-page essay that answers the following critical question:

Does Laertes or Hamlet show greater nobility of character?

Explain that essays should include:

• a clearly stated thesis which answers the critical question;

• a consideration of the foil–character relationship between Laertes and Hamlet with an explanation of how this strengthens the conclusion;

• a discussion of the three or four reasons supported with textual reference for the conclusion;

• evidence that the opposing point of view has been considered (i.e., shows open mindedness).

open-mindedness

Evaluation   *Blackline Masters #2-3*

Assess the character traits

➤ Assess students' gathering of evidence about the character's traits using *Assesing the character traits* (Blackline Master #2). According to this rubric, the assignment is worth 10 marks based on two criteria:

• identifies relevant passages from the play;

• draws plausible inferences about the character.

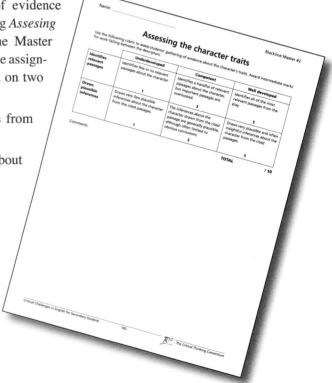

Assess the essays

➤ Assess the essays using *Assessing the conclusions* (Blackline Master #3). According to this rubric, essays are worth 15 marks based on the following criteria:

- provides convincing reasons supported by textual references;

- explains why the alternative interpretation is less plausible;

- the technical quality of the written expression is proficient.

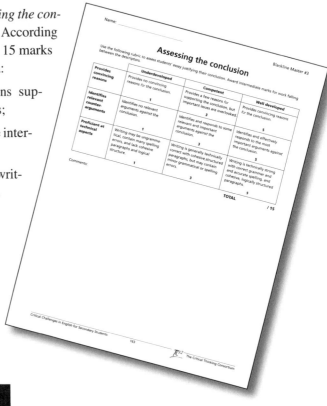

Extension

Create a soliloquy

➤ Invite students to write, in either blank verse or prose, "Laertes' soliloquy," to be inserted into the play at the end of IV, vii (when Laertes learns that his sister Ophelia's madness has led to her drowning). In this soliloquy, he ponders his present situation and his possible courses of action. Suggest that students use as a model Hamlet's "To be or not to be" soliloquy, (III, i, 56–88).

Rewrite a scene

➤ Ask students to write a paragraph describing and explaining how Hamlet would have acted in the confrontation scene with Claudius (IV, v), if he were in Laertes' situation.

Inferring character traits

Character _____

EVIDENCE Act/scene/line(s)	EVIDENCE What the character says or does	INFERENCE From this evidence, I infer that the character is . . .
I, ii, 50-56	*Asks Claudius's permission to return to his studies in France; "Dread my lord . . ."*	*respectful (of the king's authority)*

Assessing the character traits

Use the following rubric to assess students' gathering of evidence about the character's traits. Award intermediate marks for work falling between the descriptors.

	Underdeveloped	**Competent**	**Well developed**
Identifies relevant passages	Identifies few or no relevant passages about the character.	Identifies a handful of relevant passages about the character, but important passages are overlooked.	Identifies all of the most relevant passages from the play.
	1	**3**	**5**
Draws plausible inferences	Draws very few plausible inferences about the character from the cited passages.	The inferences about the character drawn from the cited passage are generally plausible, although often limited to obvious conclusions.	Draws very plausible and often insightful inferences about the character from the cited passages.
	1	**3**	**5**

TOTAL   / 10

Comments:

Assessing the conclusion

Use the following rubric to assess students' essay justifying their conclusion. Award intermediate marks for work falling between the descriptors.

	Underdeveloped	**Competent**	**Well developed**
Provides convincing reasons	Provides no convincing reasons *for* the conclusion. **1**	Provides a few reasons *for* supporting the conclusion, but important issues are overlooked. **3**	Provides convincing reasons *for* the conclusion. **5**
Identifies relevant counter-arguments	Identifies no relevant arguments *against* the conclusion. **1**	Identifies and responds to some relevant and important arguments *against* the conclusion. **3**	Identifies and effectively responds to the most important arguments *against* the conclusion. **5**
Proficient at technical aspects	Writing may be ungrammatical, contain many spelling errors, and lack cohesive paragraphs and logical structure. **1**	Writing is generally technically correct with cohesive, structured paragraphs, but may contain minor grammatical or spelling errors. **3**	Writing is technically strong with correct grammar and and accurate spelling, and cohesive, logically structured paragraphs. **5**

TOTAL   **/ 15**

Comments:

Honesty: Is it the best policy?

Critical Challenge

Critical question

Is cheating always harmful to both the individual who cheats and the society to which he or she belongs?

Overview

In this challenge, students explore the act of cheating. Andrea Chisholm's essay "The 'High' of an Honest Win" examines the question of cheating, and more particularly, whether cheating is harmful to both the individual who cheats and the society to which he or she belongs. Students complete a pre-questionnaire about their attitudes towards cheating, and then investigate more deeply what it means to cheat. They read Chisholm's essay, explore the reasons for and against cheating and write a brief essay in response to Chisholm's essay.

Objectives

Broad understanding

Students will appreciate that cheating can have widespread effects.

Requisite tools

Background knowledge
- understanding the concept of "cheating"
- understanding the merits of not cheating

Criteria for judgment
- criteria for well-supported conclusion (e.g., clearly stated position, relevant arguments, anticipates counter-arguments)

Critical thinking vocabulary

Thinking strategies
- list pros and cons
- rate strength of arguments
- template for a position paper

Habits of mind
- open-mindedness

TC^2 The Critical Thinking Consortium

Suggested Activities

Introduce focus on cheating

➤ Explain to students that this lesson focusses on an essay by Andrea Chisholm about cheating. Explain that each student will first complete an anonymous questionnaire about cheating in order to gain insight into the general attitudes about cheating held by the class. Assure students that the questionnaires will be used only for general discussion purposes and not to judge anyone.

Complete questionnaire

➤ Distribute a copy of *Questionnaire on cheating* (Blackline Master #1) to each student and give them 10 minutes to complete it. This 14-item questionnaire is designed to measure students' initial responses to assumptions and issues that Chisholm raises in her essay. Ask students to write a secret number from 100 to 1000 on the back of the questionnaire. The secret number will allow students to retrieve their questionnaire without anyone else knowing which questionnaire belonged to which student.

Compile questionnaire results

➤ Collect the completed questionnaires and—to facilitate tabulation of data—redistribute them randomly, giving one completed questionnaire to each student. Tabulate the results by reading each question and having students indicate by raising their hand the response on the questionnaire before them. Record the tally for each question on an overheard prepared from *Questionnaire results* (Blackline Master #2).

Check for understanding of results

➤ Confirm that students understand what the scores mean by asking students to interpret several of the results (e.g., If 19 of 27 responses to the comment "Everyone cheats sometimes" are "strongly agree," then what does this say about the prevalent attitude towards the frequency of cheating?). Invite students to share their reactions to the class results. Collect the questionnaires for later return to their authors.

➤ Divide students into groups of three or four, and invite them to complete *What is cheating?* (Blackline Master #3). Ask the groups to discuss whether each of the ten actions listed is an example of cheating or not. Each group will effectively compile a definition of cheating by listing the key element of each action that caused them to classify it as an example or not.

concept of cheating

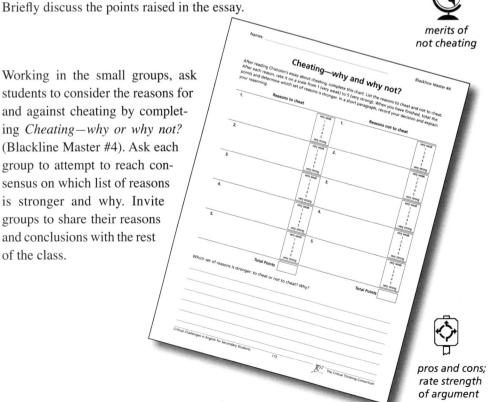

Reach consensus on definition

➤ Invite each group to write their definition—i.e., their list of the key elements—of cheating on the board. As a class, discuss the differing lists and endeavour to reach consensus on a working definition of cheating.

Session Two | Blackline Master #4

Read essay by Chisholm

➤ Ask students to read Chisholm's essay, "The 'High' of an Honest Win." Briefly discuss the points raised in the essay.

merits of not cheating

List pros and cons of cheating

➤ Working in the small groups, ask students to consider the reasons for and against cheating by completing *Cheating—why or why not?* (Blackline Master #4). Ask each group to attempt to reach consensus on which list of reasons is stronger and why. Invite groups to share their reasons and conclusions with the rest of the class.

pros and cons; rate strength of argument

Review questionnaires

➤ Using the secret numbers, return the preliminary questionnaires to students. Invite them to re-examine their original responses to the questions in Part II (items 5 to 14). Discuss open-mindedness—the willingness to reconsider one's original position in the face of new information Encourage students to share any personal revelations.

open-mindedness

Pose critical question

➤ Present the critical question:

Is cheating always harmful to both the individual who cheats and the society to which he or she belongs?

Organize response essay

➤ Ask students to compose a brief response essay that supports, modifies or refutes Chisholm's thesis. Suggest that students organize their essay according to the following structure:

template for a position paper

Paragraph 1: Briefly explain the issue, state their position on it, but do not present any reasons.

Paragraph 2: Explain and support the reasons for their position.

well-supported conclusion

Paragraph 3: Identify reasons for a counter-position. Begin this paragraph with words like "On the other hand, some people believe...." Offer any arguments that might be used to support their position against these counter-arguments.

Paragraph 4: Compose a conclusion that refers back to the arguments and their position on the issue.

Evaluation   *Blackline Masters #5-6*

Assess the rating of arguments

➤ Assess student's rating of the arguments for and against cheating using *Assessing the rating of arguments* (Blackline Master #5). According to this rubric, the assignment is worth 15 marks, based on three criteria:

• identifies credible arguments for and against cheating;

• offers plausible rating of the strength of each argument;

• justifies overall conclusion.

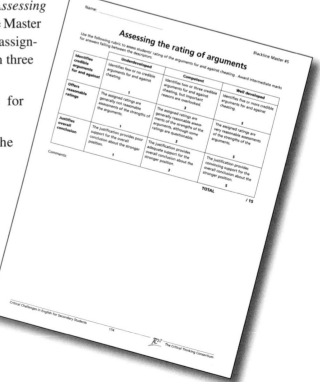

➤ Assess student response essays using *Assessing the conclusion* (Blackline Master #5). According to this rubric, the assignment is worth 15 marks, evaluated according to the following criteria:

- considers and responds to opposing reasons;

- provides convincing reasons for the conclusion;

- is technically proficient and follows required structure.

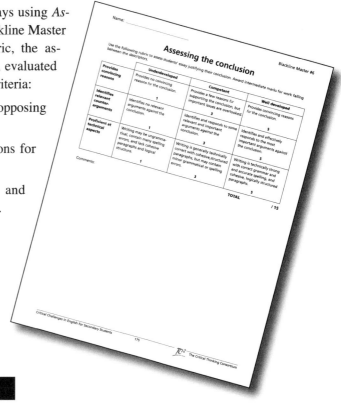

Extension

➤ Using the same tabulation procedure with the post-lesson responses, compare any changes in group results between pre- and post-lesson responses. Discuss with the class the reasons for and significance of these changes, or lack of changes.

Reference

Chisholm, Andrea. (1992). "The 'High' of An Honest Win." In *Essays: Patterns and Perspectives*. Don Mills, ON: Oxford University Press.

Questionnaire on cheating

	strongly disagree	disagree	agree	strongly agree

Part I

1. A study showed that 71 percent of students have copied homework to pass a homework check. Results would be about the same at my school.

| 1 | 2 | 3 | 4 |

2. The study showed that these same students had all attempted to find out test questions and answers from students who had previously written the test. Results would be about the same at my school.

| 1 | 2 | 3 | 4 |

3. The 71 percent of students who admitted to copying homework and attempting to find test questions and answers included many "A" students who had a reputation for being honest. Results would be about the same at my school.

| 1 | 2 | 3 | 4 |

4. These students justified their action with the reason, "It is just a survival tactic. Parents and teachers expect more from us than we can actually do." Comments would be about the same at my school.

| 1 | 2 | 3 | 4 |

Part II

5. Everyone cheats sometimes.

| 1 | 2 | 3 | 4 |

6. When lots of people are cheating, I have to cheat too.

| 1 | 2 | 3 | 4 |

7. It is not a "big deal" to cheat on something small, such as a homework check, but it is wrong to cheat when money or awards are at stake.

| 1 | 2 | 3 | 4 |

8. Getting test questions or answers from someone else is not really cheating.

| 1 | 2 | 3 | 4 |

9. A little cheating in school is a necessary survival tool.

| 1 | 2 | 3 | 4 |

10. Nothing can be done about cheating.

| 1 | 2 | 3 | 4 |

11. All cheating is wrong.

| 1 | 2 | 3 | 4 |

12. All cheating results in negative consequences.

| 1 | 2 | 3 | 4 |

13. Cheating is harmful to the person who cheats.

| 1 | 2 | 3 | 4 |

14. Cheating is harmful to society.

| 1 | 2 | 3 | 4 |

Questionnaire results

		strongly disagree	disagree	agree	strongly agree
1.	71 percent of students have copied homework.				
2.	Students had all attempted to find out test questions and answers.				
3.	Students who copied/found test questions included many "A" students who had a reputation for being honest.				
4.	Students justified their action with the reason, "It is just a survival tactic. . ."				
5.	Everyone cheats sometimes.				
6.	When lots of people are cheating, I have to cheat too.				
7.	It is not a "big deal" to cheat on something small.				
8.	Getting test questions or answers from someone else is not really cheating.				
9.	A little cheating in school is a necessary survival tool.				
10.	Nothing can be done about cheating.				
11.	All cheating is wrong.				
12.	All cheating results in negative consequences.				
13.	Cheating is harmful to the person who cheats.				
14.	Cheating is harmful to society.				

What is cheating?

Indicate whether the following actions are examples of cheating or not. Consider who is affected by the action and what the consequences could be. Identify the most important reason you use to classify each action. Use these reasons to help you formulate statements on the key elements of cheating. Record these elements in the space below the chart.

		Example of cheating		Reason for answer
1.	committing a "good" foul in a basketball game	YES	NO	
2.	asking someone who has already written a test for questions or answers	YES	NO	
3.	copying some else's homework if it's not for marks	YES	NO	
4.	"peeking" at a classmate's answers during a test	YES	NO	
5.	getting some else to write a paper for you if you return the favour some time later	YES	NO	
6.	being excused from taking a required course because you are a star college athlete	YES	NO	
7.	telling a lie so that you won't get someone else in trouble	YES	NO	
8.	watching someone cheat on a test and not reporting it	YES	NO	
9.	copying a report out of a library book	YES	NO	
10.	saying you need more time to complete an in-class essay so you can get help from someone else	YES	NO	

Key elements of cheating:

1. _____

_____

2. _____

_____

3. _____

_____

4. _____

_____

Cheating—why and why not?

After reading Chisholm's essay about cheating, complete this chart. List the reasons to cheat and not to cheat. After each reason, rate it on a scale from 1 (very weak) to 5 (very strong). When you have finished, total the points and determine which set of reasons is stronger. In a short paragraph, record your decision and explain your reasoning.

Reasons to cheat		Reasons not to cheat	
1.	very weak 1 2 3 4 5 very strong	1.	very weak 1 2 3 4 5 very strong
2.	very weak 1 2 3 4 5 very strong	2.	very weak 1 2 3 4 5 very strong
3.	very weak 1 2 3 4 5 very strong	3.	very weak 1 2 3 4 5 very strong
4.	very weak 1 2 3 4 5 very strong	4.	very weak 1 2 3 4 5 very strong
5.	very weak 1 2 3 4 5 very strong	5.	very weak 1 2 3 4 5 very strong
Total Points		**Total Points**	

Which set of reasons is stronger: to cheat or not to cheat? Why?

_____

_____

_____

_____

_____

Assessing the rating of arguments

Use the following rubric to assess students' rating of the arguments for and against cheating. Award intermediate marks for answers falling between the descriptors.

	Underdeveloped	**Competent**	**Well developed**
Identifies credible arguments for and against	Identifies few or no credible arguments for and against cheating. 1	Identifies two or three credible arguments for and against cheating, but important reasons are overlooked. 3	Identifies five or more credible arguments for and against cheating. 5
Offers reasonable ratings	The assigned ratings are generally not reasonable assessments of the strengths of the arguments. 1	The assigned ratings are generally reasonable assessments of the strengths of the arguments, although some ratings are questionable. 3	The assigned ratings are very reasonable assessments of the strengths of the arguments. 5
Justifies overall conclusion	The justification provides poor support for the overall conclusion about the stronger position. 1	The justification provides adequate support for the overall conclusion about the stronger position. 3	The justification provides convincing support for the overall conclusion about the stronger position. 5

TOTAL   **/ 15**

Comments:

Assessing the conclusion

Use the following rubric to assess students' essay justifying their conclusion. Award intermediate marks for work falling between the descriptors.

	Underdeveloped	**Competent**	**Well developed**
Provides convincing reasons	Provides no convincing reasons *for* the conclusion. **1**	Provides a few reasons *for* supporting the conclusion, but important issues are overlooked. **3**	Provides convincing reasons *for* the conclusion. **5**
Identifies relevant counter-arguments	Identifies no relevant arguments *against* the conclusion. **1**	Identifies and responds to some relevant and important arguments *against* the conclusion. **3**	Identifies and effectively responds to the most important arguments *against* the conclusion. **5**
Proficient at technical aspects	Writing may be ungrammatical, contain many spelling errors, and lack cohesive paragraphs and logical structure. **1**	Writing is generally technically correct with cohesive, structured paragraphs, but may contain minor grammatical or spelling errors. **3**	Writing is technically strong with correct grammar and and accurate spelling, and cohesive, logically structured paragraphs. **5**

TOTAL   **/ 15**

Comments:

Punctuating the lyrics

Critical Challenge

Critical task

Punctuate five sections of the song and explain the punctuation selected.

Overview

In this challenge, students consider how the Indigo Girls' song "Galileo," (or another appropriate song) written entirely in lower case letters without punctuation, presents a unique punctuation task. The song is difficult to follow on paper, and is therefore an effective demonstration of the importance of punctuation. Students listen to the song to hear punctuation clues, add the punctuation marks they detect to the text of the song lyrics, and rewrite the lyrics with punctuation added. They explain their choice of punctuation.

Objectives

Broad understanding

Punctuation contributes to clear written communication and variations in punctuation can alter meaning.

Requisite tools

Background knowledge
- knowledge of relationship between oral clues and punctuation conventions
- knowledge of rules of capitalization, end punctuation, internal punctuation (e.g., commas, semi-colon, dash)

Criteria for judgment
- criteria for effective punctuation (e.g., captures author's intentions, clarifies meaning, signals integrity of ideas, uses accepted conventions)

Critical thinking vocabulary

Thinking strategies

Habits of mind
- attention to detail

Suggested Activities

Compare oral and written communication

➤ Explain to students that punctuation and capitalization are devices to signal the intended meanings and units of thought that someone who was speaking would communicate through intonation, pauses, volume, and other aural clues. Illustrate the relationship between oral expression and punctuation by reading the following sentences with varying emphases:

- Stop, stop, stop, stop.
- Stop, stop. Stop, stop.
- Stop. Stop. Stop. Stop!

Invite students to identify the differences in the ways in which you read the segments. Ask students to suggest how each segment might be punctuated to reflect the differences.

Review punctuation rules

➤ Prior to starting, it may be useful to quickly review the basic rules of the punctuation to be used in this lesson. Establish a class set of criteria for judging when and why punctuation is needed (e.g., to clarify meaning, to recognize independent ideas).

criteria for effective punctuation

Present first part of critical task

➤ Present the first part of the critical task:

Punctuate the song.

Obtain lyrics

➤ Ask students to obtain a copy of the song lyrics. They can download a copy of "Galileo" for personal study from the indigogirls.com website. NB: Remember to adhere to the copyright restrictions posted on the website and obtain any permissions required.

Play song

➤ Play the song for the class. Advise students to listen to the natural pauses in the song's phrasing to obtain punctuation clues. Direct students to add punctuation as they read along while listening to the song. It will likely be necessary to play the song at least twice.

attention to detail

Review draft punctuated text

➤ Ask students to review the lyrics without listening to them and consider and possibly amend their punctuation of the song.

Present sections to the class

➤ Divide students into pairs or small groups to discuss their decisions about punctuation. Assign groups a portion of the song to present to the class in punctuated form. Arrange for groups to record their punctuated portion on acetate sheets. Using an overhead projector, ask students to show their punctuated lyrics to the rest of the class.

Discuss editorial choices

➤ During the presentations, ask other groups to discuss the editorial decisions made by each group. Discuss the subtleties of punctuation and observe how varying the punctuation can affect the meaning conveyed. Review the criteria for deciding whether punctuation is effective and correct.

attention to detail

Explore alternative interpretations

➤ Listen to the song once more and ask students to consider how varying the punctuation of the song produces different meanings. Conclude the lesson with a discussion about the importance of punctuation.

Present second part of critical task

➤ Present the second part of the critical task:

Explain the punctuation selected.

Assign students five short sections from the text of the song. Ask them to annotate their punctuated version of these sections with a brief explanation of how their punctuation affects interpretation and clarifies meaning.

Evaluation   *Blackline Master #1*

Assess punctuated section

➤ Evaluate students' punctuation and explanation using *Assessing punctuation* (Blackline Master #1). According to this rubric, the assignment is worth 10 marks, based on the following criteria:

• selected texts embody accepted principles of punctuation;

• provides an adequate explanation of punctuation choices in light of the aural clues and the listener's interpretation of the intended meaning.

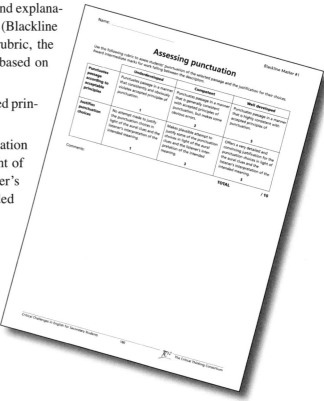

Extension

Discuss the song's message

➤ Discuss the message of the song—the desire to seek the deep truths of our lives—alluding to the references to the astronomer Galileo's discoveries concerning the workings of the universe.

Apply strategy to other texts

➤ Present students with the "free verse" text of a passage from a story or a piece of non-fiction. Read the passage to students with the author's intended pauses and emphases. Ask students to capitalize and punctuate the stripped text.

Assessing punctuation

Use the following rubric to assess students' punctuation of the selected passage and the justification for their choices. Award intermediate marks for work falling between the descriptors.

	Underdeveloped	**Competent**	**Well developed**
Punctuates passage according to acceptable principles	Punctuates passage in a manner that consistently and obviously violates accepted principles of punctuation. **1**	Punctuates passage in a manner that is generally consistent with accepted principles of punctuation, but makes some obvious errors. **3**	Punctuates passage in a manner that is highly consistent with accepted principles of punctuation. **5**
Justifies punctuation choices	No attempt made to justify the punctuation choices in light of the aural clues and the listener's interpretation of the intended meaning. **1**	Makes plausible attempt to justify some of the punctuation choices in light of the aural clues and the listener's interpretation of the intended meaning. **3**	Offers a very detailed and convincing justification for the punctuation choices in light of the aural clues and the listener's interpretation of the intended meaning. **5**

TOTAL   **/ 10**

Comments:

On the other hand

Critical Challenge

Critical task	A. Assess the success of the published rewrite of the traditional fairy tale.
	B. Rewrite a classic fairy tale from the point of view of a secondary character.
Overview	In this two-part challenge, students shift the point of view of a fairy tale to that of a secondary character and rewrite the story from this perspective. They begin by hearing a revised version of a classic fairy tale—possibly *The Frog Prince Continued* (Jon Scieszka's rewrite of "The Frog Prince") or *The True Story of the Three Little Pigs! by A. Wolf* (Jon Scieszka's rewrite of "The Three Little Pigs"). After discussing the notion of point of view and the techniques writers use to alter point of view, students identify criteria for an effective "rewrite" of a fairy tale. They use these criteria to assess the effectiveness of the published revision before they rewrite a different fairy tale.

Objectives

Broad understanding	The narrator's point of view can dramatically change a reader's perception of a story.
Requisite tools	***Background knowledge***

- familiarity with traditional and revised versions of a classic fairy tale

Criteria for judgment

- features of a successful "re-write" (e.g., believable, empathetic, inclusive of key events, imaginative, authentic tone and style)

Critical thinking vocabulary

- point of view

Thinking strategies

- data chart

Habits of mind

- role empathy

Suggested Activities

Read revised tale

➤ Read a revised version of a classic fairy tale to the class. *The Frog Prince Continued* (a rewrite of "The Frog Prince") or *The True Story of the Three Little Pigs! by A. Wolf* (a rewrite of "The Three Little Pigs"), both by Jon Scieszka, are good examples to use.

familiarity with fairy tales

Discuss point of view

➤ After reading the revised fairy tale, divide students into groups of four or five to discuss the similarities and differences between the original and the revised versions. Encourage students to explore the ranges of differences in interpretations of motive, character identification, description of events, outcome, etc., that emerge when a story is told from a secondary character's point of view. You may want to suggest that students use *Comparing the versions* (Blackline Master #1) to record the similarities and differences between the two versions. Invite students to share the results of their group's discussion with the rest of the class. Ensure that all students understand that the revised version has shifted the point of view from which the tale is normally told.

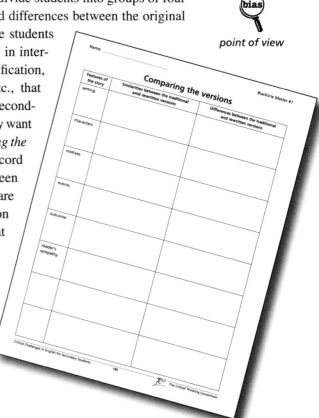

point of view

Determine criteria

➤ In a class discussion, ask students to brainstorm the key features of a successful "point of view" rewrite of a fairy tale and create a list on the chalkboard. The following criteria are especially relevant for consideration:

features of a successful re-write

- *believable*: the reinterpretation is credible/plausible;
- *empathetic*: sensitively captures another character's perspective, feelings, and outlook;
- *inclusive*: accounts for all of the events in the original tale;
- *imaginative*: offers a fresh or thoughtful reinterpretation of the character's motives and thinking;
- *authentic*: is written in the language, tone and style of the original fairy tale.

➤ After the class has discussed and agreed upon criteria for a successful rewrite, present the first critical challenge.

> *Assess the success of the published re-write of the traditional fairy tale.*

Ask students to discuss in their groups how successfully the revised fairy tale they have just heard meets these criteria. Make available a traditional version of the fairy tale for students to consult. Distribute copies of *A successful rewrite* (Blackline Master #2), or a similar activity sheet listing the criteria that the class generated, for students to use in assessing the success of the revised version of the fairy tale.

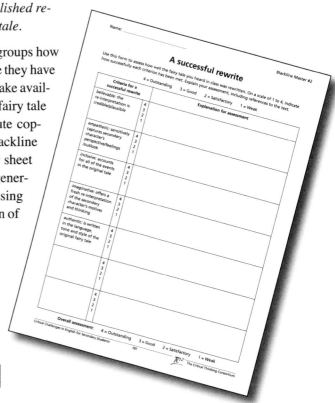

Session Two

➤ Ask students to share their assessments with the rest of the class, encouraging them to support their conclusions with references from the text.

➤ After a brief class discussion on the degree of success of the re-write of the fairy tale, present the critical task:

> *Rewrite a classic fairy tale from the point of view of a secondary character.*

Begin by brainstorming the titles of other fairy tales that might lend themselves to adaptation to the perspective of a secondary character. Decide whether all students will rewrite the same fairy tale, or whether students will make their own selection. Encourage students to study the classic version before beginning the task. Remind students to attend to the criteria for an effective rewrite as they complete the assignment.

➤ If students are familiar with the writing process—prewriting, drafting, editing, revising, publishing and presenting—suggest that they proceed through each of the steps, beginning with a prewriting exercise where they share ideas with one another in small groups prior to settling down to write a rough draft.

➤ In groups of four or five, arrange for students to read each other's revised fairy tales and to nominate which one of them is the most effective, given the agreed-upon criteria. You may wish to use *A successful rewrite* (Blackline Master #1), or a similar activity sheet listing the criteria that the class generated for students to use in assessing the most successfully rewritten fairy tale. Present each group's nomination to the entire class which will then select the three best rewritten classics.

Evaluation

Blackline Masters #3-5

Assess the comparison

➤ Assess students' comparison of the traditional and rewritten fairy tale using *Assessing the comparison* (Blackline Master #3). According to this rubric, the assignment is worth 10 marks based on two criteria:

- identifies numerous similarities and differences;

- recognizes less obvious similarities and differences.

Assess rating of published rewrite

➤ Use *Assessing "A successful rewrite"* (Blackline Master #4) to assess students' completion of Blackline Master #1. According to this rubric, the assignment is worth 10 marks based on the following criteria:

- includes relevant evidence from the story;

- supports the rating with convincing reasons.

Assess students' revised fairy tale

➤ Assess students' rewritten fairy tales using *Assessing the fairy tale* (Blackline Master #5). According to this rubric, the task is worth 25 marks based on the following criteria:

- believable in the context of the original story

- empathetic

- inclusive

- imaginative

- authentic.

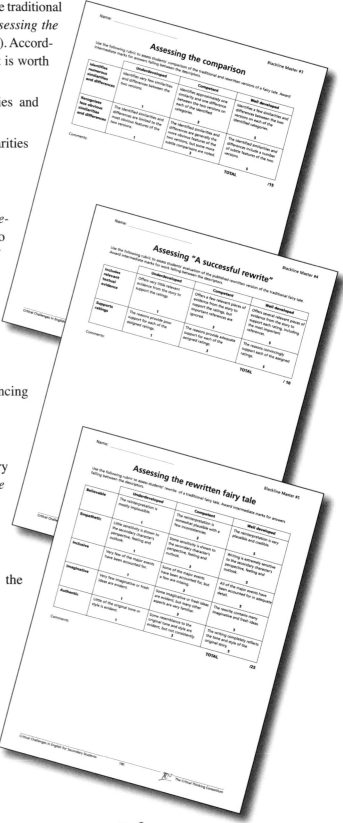

*TC*² The Critical Thinking Consortium

Extension

Illustrate the revised tales

Rewrite from an alternative perspective

Rewrite using other narrative styles

➤ Invite students to prepare an illustrated version of their fairy tale to share with their fellow students or with an elementary class.

➤ Invite students to write a continuation of a traditional fairy tale from the point of view of an alternative character.

➤ Drawing from an anthology of short stories, select and read a story which lends itself to further discussion of point of view. It may be useful to further refine students' notion of point of view to include first-person narrative, second-person narrative and omniscient narrator. Students might select a passage from the story and rewrite it from two other narrative perspectives.

References

Scieszka, Jon. Illustrated by Lane Smith. (1996). *The True Story of the Three Little Pigs! by A, Wolf.* New York: Puffin Books.

Scieszka, Jon. Illustrated by Steve Johnson. (2003). *The Frog Prince Continued.* Pine Plains, NY: Live Oak Media.

Comparing the versions

Features of the story	Similarities between the traditional amd rewritten versions	Differences between the traditional and rewritten versions
setting		
characters		
motives		
events		
outcome		
reader's sympathy		

A successful rewrite

Use this form to assess how well the fairy tale you heard in class was rewritten. On a scale of 1 to 4, indicate how successfully each criterion has been met. Explain your assessment, including references to the text.

4 = Outstanding   3 = Good   2 = Satisfactory   1 = Weak

Criteria for a successful rewrite		Explanation for assessment
believable: the re-interpretation is credible/plausible	4 3 2 1	
empathetic: sensitively captures secondary character's perspective/feelings /outlook	4 3 2 1	
inclusive: accounts for all of the events in the original tale	4 3 2 1	
imaginative: offers a fresh re-interpretation of the secondary character's motives and thinking	4 3 2 1	
authentic: is written in the language, tone and style of the original fairy tale	4 3 2 1	
	4 3 2 1	
	4 3 2 1	

Overall assessment: 4 = Outstanding   3 = Good   2 = Satisfactory   1 = Weak

Assessing the comparison

Use the following rubric to assess students' comparison of the traditional and rewritten versions of a fairy tale. Award intermediate marks for answers falling between the descriptors.

	Underdeveloped	**Competent**	**Well developed**
Identifies numerous similarities and differences	Identifies very few similarities and differences between the two versions. 1	Identifies approximately one similarity and one difference between the two versions on each of the identified categories. 3	Identifies a few similarities and differences between the two versions on each of the identified categories. 5
Recognizes less obvious similarities and differences	The identified similarities and differences are limited to the most obvious features of the two versions. 1	The identified similarities and differences are generally the more obvious features of the two versions, but some more subtle comparisons are noted. 3	The identified similarities and differences include a number of subtle features of the two versions. 5

TOTAL   **/15**

Comments:

Assessing "A successful rewrite"

Use the following rubric to assess students' evaluation of the published rewritten version of the traditional fairy tale. Award intermediate marks for work falling between the descriptors.

	Underdeveloped	Competent	Well developed
Includes relevant textual evidence	Offers very little relevant evidence from the story to support the ratings. **1**	Offers a few relevant pieces of evidence from the story to support the ratings, but important references are ignored. **3**	Offers several relevant pieces of evidence from the story to support each rating, including the most important references. **5**
Supports ratings	The reasons provide poor support for each of the assigned ratings. **1**	The reasons provide adequate support for each of the assigned ratings. **3**	The reasons convincingly support each of the assigned ratings. **5**

TOTAL   **/ 10**

Comments:

Assessing the rewritten fairy tale

Use the following rubric to assess students' rewrite of a traditional fairy tale. Award intermediate marks for answers falling between the descriptors.

	Underdeveloped	Competent	Well developed
Believable	The reinterpretation is mostly implausible. 1	The reinterpretation is somewhat plausible with a few inconsistencies. 3	The reinterpretation is very plausible and credible. 5
Empathetic	Little sensitivity is shown to the secondary character's perspective, feeling and outlook. 1	Some sensitivity is shown to the secondary character's perspective, feeling and outlook. 3	Writing is extremely sensitive to the secondary character's perspective, feeling and outlook. 5
Inclusive	Very few of the major events have been accounted for. 1	Some of the major events have been accounted for, but a few are missing. 3	All of the major events have been accounted for in adequate detail. 5
Imaginative	Very few imaginative or fresh ideas are evident. 1	Some imaginative or fresh ideas are evident, but many other aspects are very familiar. 3	The rewrite contains many imaginative and fresh ideas. 5
Authentic	Little of the original tone or style is evident. 1	Some resemblance to the original tone and style are evident, but not consistently. 3	The writing completely reflects the tone and style of the original story. 5

TOTAL   **/25**

Comments: